WORRY-FREE LIVING

WORRY-FREE LIVING

Frank Minirth, M.D.
Paul Meier, M.D.
Don Hawkins, Th.M.

THOMAS NELSON PUBLISHERS
Nashville

❖ *A Janet Thoma Book* ❖

Published in Nashville, Tennessee, by Thomas Nelson, Inc., and distributed in Canada by Lawson Falle, Ltd., Cambridge, Ontario.

Printed in the United States of America.

Unless otherwise noted, the Scripture quotations in this publication are from THE NEW KING JAMES VERSION of the Bible. Copyright © 1979, 1980, 1982, Thomas Nelson, Inc., Publishers. Scripture quotations noted TLB are from *The Living Bible* (Wheaton, Illinois: Tyndale House Publishers, 1971) and are used by permission.

Library of Congress Cataloging-in-Publication Data

Minirth, Frank B.
  Worry-free living / Frank Minirth, Paul Meier, Don Hawkins.
    p.   cm.
  Bibliography: p.

  1. Anxiety 2. Anxiety—Prevention. 3. Christian life—1960–
I. Meier, Paul D. II. Hawkins, Don. III. Title.
BF575.A6M54   1989
152.4—dc19   ISBN 0-8407-3193-0
                                                          89-2921
                                                          CIP

6 7 8 9 10 - 97 96 95 94 93 92 91 90

CONTENTS

ABOUT THE AUTHORS

Dr. Frank Minirth is a diplomate of the American Board of Psychiatry and Neurology, and along with Dr. Paul Meier, received an M.D. from the University of Arkansas Medical School and an M.A.B.S. from Dallas Theological Seminary. They are founders of the Minirth-Meier Clinic in Dallas, Texas, the second largest psychiatric clinic in the world, with associated clinics in Chicago; Los Angeles, Newport Beach, Orange, Laguna Hills, and Palm Beach, California; Little Rock, Arkansas; Longview, Fort Worth, Sherman, San Antonio, and Austin, Texas; and Washington, D.C. They have a daily call-in radio program, "The Minirth-Meier Clinic," which also features other specialists from the clinic.

Don Hawkins, who established "The Minirth-Meier Clinic" radio program, now produces a nationwide call-in program called "Life Perspectives," as well as the radio feature "The Rapha Answer." He served as a pastor for nineteen years after graduating from Dallas Theological Seminary and Southeastern Bible College.

ACKNOWLEDGMENTS

THE AUTHORS WOULD like to gratefully acknowledge those whose significant contributions helped to make *Worry-Free Living* a possibility. Specifically we are grateful for our wives, Mary Alice Minirth, Jan Meier, and Kathy Hawkins, whose encouragement has helped to reduce our personal anxiety. We are also grateful to Holly Miller for her editorial and literary expertise and labors; Janet Thoma for her administrative and editorial contributions; Susan Salmon for her editorial assistance; Bruce Barbour, who encouraged the project along; Vicky Warren and Kathy Short for many hours of labor, typing, and revising the manuscript; and the many others who contributed significantly to this material.

INTRODUCTION

LIFE ON EARTH is a brief journey. Whether that journey is a pleasant and meaningful one depends primarily on you. Popular opinion would place the responsibility for the peacefulness and pleasantness of your own individual journey on such things as your environment, your parents, your mate, your boss, good or bad luck, or even such totally ignorant things as which astrology sign you were born under. Even well-intentioned, intelligent human beings go through their brief earth journeys with unreasonable degrees of anxiety or inner emotional pain because of widespread misconceptions about who is responsible for making their own journeys peaceful, pleasant, and meaningful. Other intelligent human beings accept that responsibility for themselves (a decision involving becoming their own best friends), but are ignorant about how to do it.

Our culture is just barely coming out of the Dark Ages when it comes to good information on worry-free living. As authors, the three of us (two psychiatrists and a minister) have every intent to pass the secrets along to you so that you can help yourself to some worry-free living. After all, today is the first day of the rest of your life. Have a good trip!

Paul Meier, M.D

_____ PART ONE

The Age
of Anxiety

1.

What This Book Can (and Can't) Do for You

IF YOU WERE to ask members of our Minirth-Meier clinical team to recall the most severe case of anxiety they've ever treated, you wouldn't have long to wait for a response: Linda J.

No one should suffer the mental and physical pain that crippled Linda for more than sixteen years. When she was admitted to our Behavioral Medicine Unit at Memorial Hospital in Garland, Texas, in 1986, her high spirit was broken, her good looks had faded, and she couldn't remember a night when she had slept more than three hours. She battled migraine headaches daily and had consulted with every doctor within driving distance of her hometown in the Southeast. Our clinic was a last resort, she told us, and her treatment was to be the parting gesture of her husband who was about to file for divorce.

Tangled and dramatic, Linda's story seemed assured of an unhappy ending. After hearing it, we realized we probably couldn't save her marriage, but we certainly could help Linda. Our only regret was that she hadn't come to us sooner. Hindsight may have little value, but everyone indulges in it—even psychiatrists, therapists, and counselors. If she had come for treatment years earlier, we could have helped her that much more quickly. We also knew that if she had recognized her problem when it began—a few months after her wedding—she could have cured herself.

A book like this one might have helped her.

Linda was a southern belle. She was all style, flutter, and

drawl. She also was very bright, earned excellent grades in college, and was a natural leader, a trait made evident by her election as president of her campus sorority. She was an interesting blend of personalities. In one sense she was a woman of the eighties, at home in pinstripes and the board room; in another sense she was a throwback to an earlier era—a Scarlett O'Hara *before* the war. Only the hoop skirts and veranda were missing. In a gathering of women, Linda inevitably emerged as the eloquent spokeswoman, the assertive problem solver, and the congenial diplomat. But when men were added to the setting, her personality changed. She giggled, she blushed, and she flirted. *This is my role, isn't it?* she seemed to ask anyone who was mystified by the switch. Always a perfectionist, she played the role beautifully.

Marriage intensified her belief that women should be passive, never offer opinions, and dutifully wilt at the wisdom of their husbands. Her husband agreed.

"He's a wonderful man," Linda told us repeatedly during our early counseling sessions. "I always understood why he couldn't spend much time with me. How could he? He was working long hours to get his business off the ground. He was doing it just for us, you know. He wanted us to have all the good things in life."

Unfortunately, the "good things" didn't include his time. When the children came—first Bobby, Jr., then Leigh Ann, and finally Sandi—the demands of his office seemed to double, then triple. When he wasn't cutting important business deals on the telephone, he was traveling cross-country to close the negotiations in person. His off hours were spent presiding at one of the downtown men's service clubs and serving on two boards of local charities. His favorite project was raising funds to underwrite the football program of their college alma mater. This responsibility brought thanks and a pair of season passes from a grateful coaching staff.

"He never wanted me to go to the games because he felt one of us should be home with the children," explained Linda, defensively. "Bob has always put his family first. But how could I object to his using the tickets? He certainly deserved some fun after working so hard for us all week."

When he was home, he dominated her. He rarely asked her

opinion, seldom solicited her advice, and seemed insensitive to her needs and feelings. If she hinted that she was lonely, he would remind her of the sacrifices he made for her comfort. Didn't she wear designer clothes? Didn't she drive a new car? And how about that membership in the local country club? He surely had no time for golf. It was all for her. Feeling guilty for mentioning the loneliness, she vowed it would never come up in conversation again. And it never did.

Because anxiety hadn't been a problem for Linda as a young girl, she didn't recognize its early signs. "I'm just a little uptight," she'd say to friends who voiced concern about her tired appearance. "High-strung, I guess," she'd concede with a shrug.

The migraine headaches began soon after the birth of Bobby, Jr. They were blamed at first on her lack of sleep—"Bobby is such a fussy baby," she assured everyone—and she predicted they'd disappear as soon as teething time was over. But they didn't. When they became unbearable, she consulted a local doctor who gave her little more than a prescription for tranquilizers, a message to "Say hi to Bob for me," and a friendly chuck on the chin.

By the time her third child was born, she was housebound. Her mild tranquilizers had been upgraded to addictive drugs. Her occasional "jitters" had exploded into violent panic attacks complete with pounding heart, gasping breath, and drenching cold sweats. She visited doctor after doctor and endured test after test. The doctors were sympathetic, and their tests were negative. There was no physical reason for her misery. A psychiatrist concluded that something certainly was wrong, but he chose to treat her symptoms rather than dig for the source of her problem.

"It was all my fault," Linda explained during our first therapy session. "Poor Bob was juggling the business, trying to fulfill his obligations to the church, run his service club, and work for the alumni association. I was no help at all. Looking back, I can see now why he reached out to another woman. Our sex life was nonexistent, we never entertained, and I spent most of the time in my room, too weak to come downstairs."

The decision for Linda to fly to Texas for treatment at our clinic was as much her husband's as hers. It was a last-ditch, we've-tried-everything-else choice designed to ease both her pain and his conscience. They admitted that they held out little hope for success, but what did they have to lose?

When Linda sheepishly asked Bob to make the arrangements for the trip, she explained that she had heard one of our "Clinic" broadcasts when agoraphobia was the topic of discussion. The symptoms of this severe anxiety disorder—chest pains, dizziness, fear of leaving the house—had sounded surprisingly familiar. Was it worth looking into? Did she dare hope that someone finally could help her?

Bob agreed to call us. When he did, he explained Linda's condition and then added his personal reason for wanting treatment for his wife. A divorce was inevitable, he confided flatly, and he was afraid that Linda might become worse after he left home. He had no regrets about ending the marriage—sixteen years with an invalid was enough for anyone to endure, thank you, but he didn't need the "guilt trip" that would accompany a suicide attempt. He had no interest in her health nor in her future, other than not being responsible for the first and not playing a role in the second.

Yes, Help Is Available

It took several days of sophisticated tests to confirm the preliminary diagnosis we made during our first in-depth talk with Linda. Our conclusion? Severe anxiety.

Such an opinion might seem like a gross understatement. For a team of psychiatrists, psychologists, and therapists to huddle over charts and notes for days and then to announce that Linda J. was anxious, even *severely* anxious, may smack of oversimplification. Even her friends at the country club could have come up with something more complicated than that. They would certainly have described her condition in trendier terms: "Linda? We've hardly seen her since she had her *nervous breakdown*," they might say. (To set the record straight, in our combined forty years of medical practice we've never seen nerves "break down.") Classmates of her children would make an equally dramatic judgment: "Poor Bobby, Leigh Ann, and Sandi. Their mom is a real *basket case*."

The truth is that our diagnosis was right on target. Unfortunately, few people realize how serious anxiety can be or how it can progress to a state of disability or that it currently is the number one mental health disorder in America. The confusion is understandable. Anxiety comes in so many disguises and degrees that it defies labeling. To one person it may mean a mild case of "butterflies," while to another, it might surface as red blotches on the neck, a tongue-tied response, or a bout with heartburn. It can be positive or negative, mild or severe, an energy motivator or an enthusiasm eliminator. It's similar to, but not the same as, fear, depression, stress, worry, and burnout. It can cause one person to excel and another to fail. It can work for you or against you, depending on whether you harness it or ignore it. In its most severe state, it even can kill. Linda J. came close to being one of its victims.

As doctors, we deal with anxiety in all its forms and degrees every day. Our staff of seventy-plus professionals, located in a network of clinics across the country, treats more cases of anxiety than any other type of mental disorder. Few are as severe as Linda J.'s, but all share common elements.

- First, anxiety is treatable, often preventable, and even curable.
- Second, if recognized quickly, anxiety can be dealt with painlessly, often within minutes, and without any professional help.
- Third, anxiety can be used as a positive tool, much like a smoke alarm, to alert you to potential danger. When the alarm sounds, you must look for the source of the heat and carefully douse it.
- Finally, if you learn to read and interpret anxiety's signs, you can improve the mental health not only of yourself but of those around you.

How? That's what this book is all about. We'll show you first how to overcome anxiety and then how to prevent it from recurring.

Anxiety isn't a new topic, and we're not the first professionals to write about it. However, our approach is unique. Unlike many physicians who look at anxiety disorders from one angle or another, we examine them from three distinct perspectives. Two of us are medical doctors who have specialized in psychiatry; the third is a pastor with theological training and nineteen years of experience in counseling and administration. With that diversity in training, we and our staff are able to take a comprehensive approach to anxiety, turning it inside out and scrutinizing it from medical, psychological, and biblical points of view.

The purpose of this book is to share with you what we've learned. By drawing from our daily experiences with patients, we'll show you how to apply several simple principles. We'll provide insights into how anxiety can grab hold of you, grow, and eventually control you. Then we'll walk you through the practical steps we've devised to cope with, overcome, and prevent anxiety.

Besides boosting your awareness of the causes and symptoms of anxiety, we'll point out how the disorder relates to personality types. We'll help you figure out if you're a prime candidate for anxiety, and then we'll introduce you to the subtle warning signs and tell you what to do about them. You'll make rounds with us in the hospital, sit with us in the therapy room, visit our daily radio broadcasts, and meet several patients who have undergone successful treatment. Details of their cases will be taken directly from our files, although their identities will remain confidential and some cases will be composites of several patients. Scattered throughout the book will be several self-quizzes to help you determine how healthy your lifestyle is, the level of your coping skills, and how good a friend you are.

Of course, no book is a cure-all. At some point, if anxiety is so severe that self-help techniques aren't effective, professional counseling should be considered. How do you know when that point has been reached? We'll talk about the indicators, and we'll also discuss what you can expect from therapy. The advantages of hospitalization over outpatient care and the differences between Christian and non-Christian counseling will be explained.

Just as vibrant physical health depends to a great extent on prevention and common sense, so does good mental health. An anxiety disorder as severe as Linda J.'s didn't occur overnight, but was rooted in her earliest complaints of headaches and fatigue. If she had known how to deal with those minor discomforts when they first sounded the alarm, she would have been spared sixteen years of anguish. As it was, seven weeks in the hospital and many months of out-patient follow-up counseling were needed to completely restore her to the competent, outgoing, attractive woman she had been before her marriage. The weeks in our Behavioral Medicine Unit were difficult ones for her because she had to work her way through three sets of emotions. First, she had to break through her defenses and denial in order to air her persistent guilt; then, she had to learn how to forgive. Depression plagued her along the way, but she was able to overcome it and emerge as a wholly healed woman, who knew how to live a worry-free life.

Here's how she did it.

Fanning the Flames

Since the majority of depressions are caused by hidden anger, our clinical team suspected that Linda was bitterly enraged with someone. But whom?

"Bob was always so wonderful to me," she said once too often during a therapy session. "I really don't begrudge him a happy second marriage. If I hadn't failed him by being sick all those years he never would have been unfaithful. He deserves a wife who can be more of a companion to him. No, of course I'm not angry with Bob. I have no right to be."

As her denials continued, so did her headaches and insomnia. Repeatedly, we gently urged her to look at the truth. "Bob never helped you with the children," we reminded her. "He seldom was home; he wasn't sensitive to your needs; he didn't try to tune in to your feelings; he had an affair and never apologized for it. Now he's going to leave you."

She didn't want to hear it. Her denials became more heated. Her anxiety became noticeably heightened every time we dared to suggest that Bob had let her down. She argued that *she* had been the guilty one, not Bob. It had all been *her* fault.

"But if he was such a good husband, why didn't he take you out more often before you became sick?" we challenged. "Why did he prefer to spend weekend after weekend traveling with the football team? What was he trying to prove? Who was he trying to impress? After his business became so successful, why didn't he delegate some of the management responsibilities to one of his vice presidents so he could enjoy his children? Why did he accept appointments to church boards when he couldn't find the time to attend Sunday school with his family?"

The purpose of this probing wasn't to make Linda more miserable than she already was, and it wasn't to add to the problems in her already troubled marriage. We knew if she was ever to be free of her crippling anxiety, she had to face her hidden anger, admit its presence, and then rid herself of it. We didn't create the anger, we only drew attention to it. Unfortunately, it had been there for years, held carefully under wraps by Linda herself. And as her anger had increased, so had the burden of repressing it.

Finally, the floodgates opened. The rage that she had worked so hard to suppress surfaced and exploded. Yes, she resented her husband, she told us with emotion twisting her face and tightening the pitch of her voice. Yes, she felt shortchanged, neglected, and stifled. Yes, she saw now that her husband had manipulated her traditional beliefs and had used them to keep her in his shadow. He had stripped her of her confidence and had killed her desire to make a contribution. He had denied her the joy of a balanced, give-and-take marital relationship.

She cried, she screamed, she pounded her bed, and she beat on the walls of her hospital room. She threatened to get even by suing him. Her rage burned out of control for days as the long-repressed memories reared up to fan the flames. When other patients on the floor complained of the commotion, we moved her to the end of the hall where she wouldn't disturb anyone.

These were the most difficult days of her hospitalization. Yet they were necessary to her recovery. She had taken an essential step in her healing process. At last she was ready to move on.

"You have to forgive your husband," we told her.

"What? After all the pain he's caused me?" she retorted defiantly. "I couldn't forgive him if I wanted to, which I don't."

We explained that while Bob might not deserve her forgiveness, she had to give it to him for her own sake. She would never be free to enjoy her life until she had put her anger to rest. Doling out justice or "getting even" wasn't her responsibility. The urge to take matters into her own hands would only lead to vengeful thoughts and hateful actions that would disrupt her healing and produce bitterness. She simply had to let go.

As a committed Christian, Linda was open to the authority of Scripture, so we frequently cited relevant passages. "Remember when God told us to 'Be angry, and do not sin: do not let the sun go down on your wrath'?" we asked her.[1] "He's telling us that it's not a sin to be angry, but it is a sin to hold onto anger and to nurture it. You didn't realize it, but you've been doing that for sixteen years. Now it's time to follow God's advice: 'Let all bitterness, wrath, anger, clamor, and evil speaking be put away from you, with all malice.' "[2]

It is true that angry feelings may originate from sinful motives of selfishness or self-centeredness. Certainly most anger is not righteous indignation. However, if anger is present, then better to admit it and be honest and deal with it than to deny its presence.

She understood, although full acceptance came only after hours of discussion. She seemed to take one step forward and two steps back as she wrestled with her feelings. Her intellect told her she had to forgive, yet her emotions still wanted to even the score. She fantasized about publicly embarrassing Bob by exposing his infidelity to all the people who held him in high esteem. She even planned the dialogue she would use when she approached the civic group that had honored her husband as "Christian Businessman of the Year." She played out the scene that would result when she confronted Bob with his acts of mental cruelty and hypocrisy. As her anger was rekindled, the pain returned, and she finally could see that our counsel was correct and consistent with God's plan. She knew what she had to do. She forgave.

Her physical recovery began almost immediately. She began sleeping through the night without the inducement of tranquilizers. Her headaches eased, became less frequent, and eventually stopped altogether. Her appetite returned, and her interest in her appearance was revived. Her natural beauty, southern grace, and charm were still intact. Only the hoop skirts were gone forever.

A storybook ending to this case would have Linda and Bob reconciling their problems and driving off into the sunset in Bob's late-model luxury van. But this was no fictional story, and Bob was hardly a Hollywood hero. We contacted him by telephone and updated him on Linda's recovery. We invited him to come to the clinic and participate in the final therapy sessions. Linda had assured us that she was willing to rebuild her marriage if he would agree to a more balanced foundation. Bob refused. Divorce papers had been filed, he told us, and his plans to remarry were firm.

Still, the story had a happy ending.

Linda completed her treatment with us and went home to start her new life as a single mother. We put her in contact with a counselor in her area, and she saw him regularly for several months. She built a warm, loving network of friends that supported her in her difficult single mother/wage earner role. Within weeks of her dismissal from the hospital, she stopped taking the mild medication we had prescribed. She no longer needed it.

We still keep in touch with Linda. She's visited us twice now, more as a friend than as a former patient. Although she has learned not to indulge in "what if" and "if only" games, she can't deny her feelings. That's a lesson she learned from us. Life is wonderful, and she's sorry she missed a sixteen-year chunk of it. She regrets that she waited so long, that she didn't find help sooner, and that she didn't help herself when self-help was all she needed.

We're sorry too. A book about worry-free living might have made the difference.

We hope it does.

PART TWO

How to Overcome Anxiety

2.

The Hidden Emotion in "The Age of Anxiety"

IF YOU WERE to ask ten people to tell you what anxiety is, you'd probably get ten different answers, and all of them would be wrong.

"Anxiety? It's when I pace the floor half the night because I can't sleep," is a familiar complaint.

"It's a restlessness when I can't sit still, but at the same time I can't concentrate long enough to get anything done."

"A pain in the neck, that's what it is," is a favorite. "It starts in my shoulders and moves down my neck. Nothing seems to help it go away."

All good answers . . . but all wrong. Instead of being *definitions* of anxiety, these are *characteristics* of anxiety. They're descriptions of how anxiety presents itself in certain people. Anxiety isn't insomnia, but it can cause insomnia. Anxiety isn't restlessness, but it can cause uneasy, agitated feelings. Anxiety isn't a pain in the neck—at least not in the literal sense—but it certainly can cause one.

So what *is* anxiety? You can't successfully learn how to overcome anxiety unless you first understand exactly what it is. We define it this way: It's an emotion that a person experiences in the face of a perceived threat or a danger. We say "perceived" because the danger can be real or imagined. If the danger is real, anxiety can serve as a positive warning. It's a sort of internal red flag and siren system. If the danger is imagined, anxiety is negative baggage that weighs a person down, saps his energy, and leaves him ineffective. In either case, whether the danger is real or imagined, the anxiety and all of its symptoms are absolutely real, and they surface as feelings of uneasiness, apprehension, dread, concern, tension, restlessness, and worry. Over a period of time these feelings can burden the body until insomnia, lack of concentration, pain, and other problems result. Sometimes the anxious person senses pending misfortune or disaster and suffers the double dilemma of depression *and* anxiety because of it.

Anxiety versus Fear

"I'm anxious about tomorrow's job interview."
"I'm anxious about my algebra test."
No, you're really not. You're actually *fearful* about tomorrow's job interview, and you're *afraid* of your upcoming algebra test.
Many of us diagnose ourselves as being anxious when what we really mean is that we feel fear. Often people use the words "anxiety" and "fear" interchangeably without realizing that a shade of difference exists between them. Uncertainty is a key element of anxiety, but not of fear. If you know what you're worried about, you're experiencing fear. If you're suffering from uneasiness and tension but you don't know why, that's anxiety. True anxiety is being afraid but having no idea what it is that you fear.
In his book *The Meaning of Anxiety,* Rollo May gives an example of a college student walking to the dentist's office to have a tooth extracted. On his way, the student passes a favorite professor he knows well from class and from his campus activities. Even though they exchange glances face to face, the professor doesn't smile, say a word, or acknowledge the student. Anxiety sets in. *Am I so unimportant that he doesn't recognize me outside of the classroom? Is he angry at me? Maybe I've disappointed him in some way.*
The anxiety is pushed to the background when the student sits in the dentist's chair. He feels intense fear as the dentist probes in his mouth, injects the anesthetic, then reaches for the instrument to pull the tooth. Although the fear is much stronger than the anxiety, it disappears as soon as the tooth is out and he is on his way home. But the anxiety remains—lurking and gnawing during his waking

hours and slipping in and out of his troubled dreams at night. It's not as concentrated as the fear he experienced, but it's on a deeper level. Why he suffers from it is unknown. The perceived snub may threaten his sense of self-esteem *(Am I so unimportant that he doesn't recognize me?)*, or it may jolt his confidence *(Is he angry at me?)*, or it may make him feel guilty *(Maybe I've disappointed him)*.[1]

Anxiety and fear are tightly linked. As Christian psychiatrists we believe that a person becomes anxious when he is afraid to look at a negative emotion inside of him. The emotion could be anger, guilt, lust, envy, greed, resentment, or some other less-than-positive motive. Rather than face the emotion, he buries it, denies it, ignores it, and refuses to let it surface and be seen. God knows better. In His infinite wisdom He wants each of us to examine our emotions. To deny our true feelings is to deceive ourselves. Deceit is wrong; it's a lie. The Holy Spirit uses anxiety to tug at our attention and to tell us that something needs to be aired. Anxiety becomes similar to a smoke signal that alerts us to a problem smoldering under the surface.

The reason that the professor didn't acknowledge his student in the scenario we described earlier isn't important. It could be that the professor was the absent-minded type and his mind was a million miles away. Or maybe he wasn't wearing his glasses and couldn't see the young man. What is more important is the way the student reacted to the snub. He didn't brush it off, but he let it eat away at him. His anxiety was sending up red flares to let him know that he had a buried emotion—maybe insecurity, maybe guilt—that he needed to look at and deal with.

People are afraid of the truth. We once asked our staff of counselors to estimate how many of their patients come to our clinic to learn the truth about themselves so that they can do something to correct whatever is wrong. The therapists' best guesstimate was that only 25 percent of all Minirth-Meier clients want to find out the truth, and even fewer want to deal with it. Most patients visit the clinic looking for quick and easy solutions. They want a pill to make their anxiety go away. Or they want a counselor to listen to their problems and then blame the problems on someone else. The last thing a patient wants to hear is that his own anger or guilt or jealousy is the source of his anxiety and that he is responsible for getting rid of the negative emotion.

Too often people think the way to handle anxiety is to deny it, fight it, conquer it, or drug it. A more successful approach is to bring its source to the surface, look at it, understand it, and do something about it. The counselor can offer direction, insights, support, and advice, but only the patient can decide what to do with the help once it is given to him. We said in chapter 1 that anxiety is a curable disorder. This is true *if*—and this is important—*if* the anxious person is willing to take responsibility for his cure.

Anxiety and Depression

Just as people confuse anxiety and fear, so do they have trouble distinguishing between anxiety and depression. Here's the difference: Anxiety is more linked to the future, and depression is connected more directly with the past. Or, put another way, *anxiety is the future superimposed on the present,* and *depression is the past superimposed on the present.* This statement may be an oversimplification since a definite element of past emotion is hidden in anxiety. However, the oversimplified distinction has helped many people to understand and to face both anxiety and depression. For that reason, we continue to use it whenever we explain to laypeople the link between the two.

As an example, we could cite the case of the woman who suffers *anxiety* when she worries that something may be going wrong with her marriage. It might not have happened yet, but she senses that all is not well, and she anticipates the worst. The *depression* comes later, after her marriage has ended in divorce. She grieves about its failure, and she can't overcome the feeling of tremendous loss.

Both anxiety and depression are normal reactions that everyone experiences in life. They can become abnormal if they continue for an extended period or if they cause a person to lose control of his life or if they prompt a person to hurt himself or someone else.

To understand better how fear, anxiety, and depression relate, let's look at the file of Matt W., a graduate student who came to us several years ago for treatment of depression. Like so many depressed people, Matt also was anxious. He complained that he was distracted (the biblical word for anxiety is *merizo* which translates as "distraction"), felt little interest in his studies, and was in a constant state of agitation. Most bothersome were the migraine headaches and the insomnia. When we pressed him for details about his symptoms, we weren't surprised to hear he was getting only four hours of rest a night. (An anxious person generally has problems getting to sleep. A depressed person easily "escapes" into sleep but then wakes up in the middle of the night and can't get back to sleep.)

"Are you angry at anyone?" we asked Matt.

He shook his head no.

"Do you have guilt feelings about something?"

"No."

Medically there was nothing wrong with him. As standard practice we always give a complete physical examination to all patients who enter counseling. Matt had no chemical imbalance or deficiency that would cause him to be so uptight and depressed.

More questions. Was he worried about his school work? How about his relationship with his parents? Did they communicate often and openly? He willingly answered our questions, but nothing gave us insights as to what was at the core of his depression and anxiety. We knew, since he was struggling with depression, that his problem was linked to something in his past, which was still bothering him in the present. We knew, since he suffered from anxiety, that he was afraid to look at some negative emotion buried inside of him. But what was it? Our questions weren't reaping any helpful answers.

"Here's what we want you to do," we suggested. "We want you to keep a pad and pencil by your bed and record every dream you have during the next week. Write down your dream as soon as you wake up, even if it's in the middle of the night, before your brain can repress it. Bring the list to our next counseling session."

He was more confused than ever when he walked into our office the following Thursday. He understood that people often dream about what is bothering them subconsciously, and he knew that God sometimes teaches insightful lessons through dreams. But that didn't help him make any sense out of what he called the "crazy little drama" that had replayed itself three times during the previous week.

"Tell us about it," we said.

"It's always the same," he explained. "I'm hitchhiking along a dirt road out in the country. A car approaches with a man in the driver's seat and a woman sitting next to him. But this is no ordinary car; in fact, it's nothing more than a frame with a steering wheel and engine. No body at all! I wave to the couple, and they pick me up. I climb into the back seat, and as we drive down the road we hit a bump and the husband falls out of the car. I scramble into the front seat and slip behind the wheel. The woman and I continue to drive down the road, now with the husband running along behind us. Finally he catches up, I stop and get out, he takes the wheel again, and the two of them go off together."

He looked at us and shrugged. "Crazy, huh?"

We assured him that what he had just told us was the key to his depression and his anxiety. It was anything but "crazy."

"You've had an affair," we said. "It's over now, but you feel a lot of guilt about it. Even though the affair is a part of the past, you can't let go of it."

He agreed that he had been sexually involved with a woman about six months earlier, but he had ended the relationship and hadn't given it much thought since then. However, he admitted that his headaches and insomnia had begun to bother him at precisely the same time. With that clue, we felt sure we were on the right track.

"I needed an apartment close to the university," he explained. "I rented three rooms from a married couple. I never intended to get involved with the woman, but the marriage wasn't happy, she was lonesome, and we had a lot of time together when I was home studying and the husband was at work. The relationship only lasted a few weeks; then I moved out and haven't seen either of them since."

We pointed out the similarity between his dream and the experience he had just described. He had joined the couple for a brief time: in reality it had been for a few weeks; in the dream it had been for a few miles down a dirt road. The car, without a body, had no substance and offered no security for the passengers . . . much like the couple's marriage. For a while the couple and Matt were a threesome until Matt took the husband's place in the driver's seat and in the marriage. When the three-way relationship was over, each was where he was at the beginning; Matt was alone, and the husband and wife were united.

"It's so obvious now," said Matt after we explained the connection. "But if I feel guilt about this, why don't I know it?"

We explained that his mind had used a defense mechanism called rationalization to cover his guilt. His brain had told him that he had done nothing wrong, the marriage was shaky anyway, the husband had never found out about the relationship, Matt and the wife had never been in love, and the whole affair had lasted a very short time. No harm done, his brain insisted. But the repressed feeling of guilt wouldn't go away. While Matt knew he hadn't caused the problems in the marriage, he knew in his heart that he had added to the trouble. He had taken advantage of the unhappy situation to gratify his own lust, and he was ashamed.

Identifying a hidden emotion is an important first step in overcoming anxiety, but the work of counselor and patient isn't done yet. Remember, most patients don't want to face the truth, and identifying a hidden emotion such as guilt involves facing the truth. Neither do patients want to do anything about the truth once it's been aired. What prompts them to see a counselor is not the desire to uncover negative feelings, but to get a quick fix for the discomfort that those negative feelings cause.

Many non-Christian therapists put their clients in touch with hidden emotions, encourage them to ventilate these emotions, and then conclude the treatment. The patients are healthier because the stress of repressing their negative feelings is gone. They've aired their anger, jealousy, lust, guilt, or whatever was causing the problem. But an important step is missing.

This next step is forgiveness. What is forgiveness? Perhaps it is easier to explain what it is *not*. Forgiveness is *not* pretending something wrong didn't happen to us. Nor is it going to the other extreme and taking vengeance into our own hands. Forgiveness is not a matter of "forgive and forget." As we shall see throughout this book, memories are indelibly etched in the biochemical pathways of our brains. Often we are conscious of them, although sometimes they are "stored" in our subconscious minds where they can be called into the conscious whenever we choose to summon them. At other times they are in our unconscious and are almost impossible to retrieve. Nonetheless, they have a drastic effect on our emotions and lives.

Forgiveness is becoming aware of our anger toward someone, then choosing not to hold the offense against the person. It is deciding not to call up the memory of the offense, not to dwell on it, not to look for opportunities to take revenge.

In effect, this principle is illustrated in an event which took place annually in the life of Israel in the Old Testament. It was a tradition in those days to offer a ceremonial sacrifice by investing a "scapegoat" with all the wrongs done by the Israelites and then leading the animal into the wilderness. The scapegoat was taken to such a remote location that it would be impossible for it ever to rejoin the Israelite camp. This explains why the biblical word for *forgiveness,* used in both the Old and New Testaments, translates as "sending the offense away." In the New Testament this same principle is dramatically illustrated when Christ assumes the burden of human sin and makes the ultimate sacrifice of dying for our sin on the cross. He assures our forgiveness by taking our offenses away.

Today, when we choose to forgive an individual, whether for an insignificant slight or for a major offense, we are "sending away" that offense. This "sending away" is exactly what our patient, Matt W., had to do to be truly healed of his depression. He had to forgive himself. Once he realized that he was struggling with deep feelings of guilt, he had to admit his mistake and then learn to "send away" his sin. He could never undo what had happened, but he could seek forgiveness and continue with his life. The forgiveness step enabled him to get better more quickly and stay healthier longer.

The Christian Advantage

Unlike most of our patients, Matt wasn't a Christian. Although we are Christian psychiatrists and counselors, a faith in Jesus Christ is not a prerequisite for treatment at our clinic. In our years of practice we have treated persons of all religions and some persons who claim to have no faith at all. Many of these people respond well to treatment and recover fully. Still, we believe by comparison, Christians have a very real advantage in counseling. They have an additional power system that gives support and strength during anxious times. This Christian advantage is three-pronged:

- Christians can rely on the Word of God as the final authority to direct their behavior. God has told us what is right and wrong, so we don't have to wade through dozens of philosophies trying to determine what we should or shouldn't do. The Bible is our guidebook, and the rules are clearly stated, although some people might not want to remember some of them, like "Thou shalt not commit adultery," or "Thou shalt not covet."

- Christians have a built-in booster system to help them conquer problems. Each person is responsible for his own actions, of course, but he has the presence of God in him for additional support. Anxiety doesn't disappear when someone becomes a Christian, but the anxious Christian (yes, Christians *do* get anxious) gains tremendous strength to deal with his problems.

- Christians have God's assurance of forgiveness. This is stated in a variety of ways in a number of places: "If we confess our sins to him, he can be depended on to forgive us and to cleanse us from every wrong."[2] The idea of having our offenses "taken away" is promised in Psalm 103: "As far as the east is from the west, / So far has He removed our transgressions from us."[3] We also know that God loves us in spite of any backsliding we might do as we struggle to get on track. "I am still not all I should be but I am bringing all my energies to bear on this one thing: forgettng the past and looking forward to what lies ahead. . . ."[4]

Occasionally non-Christians ask us how they can know God's forgiveness. The answer is simple, and you can apply it in your life. First, realize you are a sinner and you have done wrong (see Romans 3:23). Second, realize that Jesus Christ, God's perfect Son, died on the cross in payment for your sins (see Romans 6:23). Finally, trust Jesus Christ as your Savior (see John 1:12). You might verbalize your faith in a prayer such as: "Lord, Jesus, I am inviting you into my life. I know I am a sinner; I know you died for me, and right now I'm trusting you as my Savior."

One of the old hymns of the faith put it this way:

> Just as I am—Thou wilt receive,
> Wilt welcome, pardon, cleanse, relieve;
> Because Thy promise, I believe,
> O Lamb of God, I come! I come![5]

For many of you reading this book, this step may be the most important you ever take in overcoming anxiety.

Join the Club!

Each of us has endured feelings of depression, and all of us have suffered the discomforts of anxiety. Join the club! If anxiety is an epidemic, no letup is in sight. In fact, this has been called the Age of Anxiety.

If depression and anxiety are inevitable for many, is worry-free living even possible? Yes, although for most people it will always remain a goal, not an achievement. The secret is to work steadfastly toward the goal. That was the apostle Paul's philosophy. After he told the Philippians to forget the past and look forward to what lies ahead, he shared his own game plan: "I press toward the goal for the prize of the upward call of God in Christ Jesus."[6] A worry-free life is a more godly life.

In pressing toward the goal of worry-free living, it is helpful to know the obstacles in the way of success. There are many; there always have been, and there always will be. Anxiety has been around since Abraham fretted about his gloomy future without heirs. It's still with us, still shrouded in mystery, still hidden by defense mechanisms, still complicated by unhealthy lifestyles, and still misunderstood by people who don't want to look at the truth about themselves. Truth is the antidote for anxiety, truth sets us free, and the first step in getting to the truth is dispelling the anxiety myths that have been with us for generations. Let's look at eight of them.

3.

Eight Myths: "You'll Get Over It"

"UPTIGHT? MUST BE midlife crisis. Give it time. It'll go away."

"Worried? But you're a Christian! Christians don't worry."

"Nervous? You'll get over it."

"High-strung? You probably inherited it from your mother."

"Jittery? Straighten up. You know the old saying, 'When the going gets tough, the tough get going.' You've got to learn to hang in there."

Besides being the most common mental health disorder in America, anxiety has a second distinction: It's the most commonly misunderstood. A Gallup poll once indicated that at least 30 to 40 percent of all Americans experience some discomfort from anxiety, and about 15 million are treated professionally for it. As we pointed out in chapter 2, we all suffer anxiety in various degrees at various times, but few of us deal with it honestly and get rid of it permanently. Instead, we deny it, make excuses for it, pass it off as a temporary condition, are embarrassed by it, and blame it on our genes, our biological cycle, our age, our poor health, and our poor mothers.

If truth is the antidote for anxiety, let's set the record straight. Let's examine and dispel eight of the most common misconceptions about the problem.

"Bad Genes"

Blaming anxiety on the family tree is a cop-out. You can't inherit anxiety, although you can inherit the way your body exhibits it.

For example, if the fictional father-and-son law partnership of Smith and Smith suffers a severe financial setback, Smith, Sr., might become very nervous, develop an ulcer, and require treatment. Why? Maybe it goes back to his childhood during the Great Depression. Maybe he overreacts because he's subconsciously panicked at the thought of enduring the kind of poverty his parents endured. Whatever the case, his son, Smith, Jr., doesn't share the fear, the memories, or the anxiety. Consequently, Junior adopts a more laid-back, whatever-will-be-will-be attitude. Same situation, different reaction. No inherited anxiety.

The following year, business is on the upswing, and Dad Smith is thriving under the financial security of a heavy caseload. Junior, however, buckles under the pressure and develops an ulcer. Same situation, different response, with one noteworthy similarity. When anxiety presents itself in father and son (for whatever reason), it shows in the same way—ulcers. Genetically the family members share a vulnerability to stomach problems. In another family the physical weakness might be the heart and result in angina, or it might be the digestive system and result in colitis.

Some studies have suggested that a tendency toward worrying can be passed from one generation to another. We believe this is impossible to prove since many children of severely anxious parents never develop serious anxiety. However, if several children live in a stressful family environment during key periods of their development, they may all suffer anxiety. This anxiety won't be caused by the genetic makeup they share, but by the situation they share. An adopted brother might develop the same anxiety. The anxiety might show itself one way among the natural brothers and sisters—stuttering, hives, headaches—and another way in the adopted child.

Just as our brain chemistry doesn't determine if we will be anxious, neither does it determine how happy or how wise we will be. People who are unhappy and nervous have chosen not to learn how to handle their emotions. They may not be responsible for the situations they must react to, but they are responsible for their reactions. Confusing? Let's look at it a different way.

More than twenty years ago, the Homes and Rahe stress chart was developed to show how much of a bearing certain events have on our lives. Each major event was given a point value—in life change units—that ranges from 100 for the death of a spouse to 11 for a minor law violation. Researchers have projected that anyone who tallies 200 or more of these units in a year is a likely candidate for a psychiatric disorder or a medical problem.

The Stress of Adjusting to Change

Events	Scale of Impact
Death of a spouse	100
Divorce	73
Marital separation	65
Jail term	63
Death of a close family member	63
Personal injury or illness	53
Marriage	50
Fired at work	47
Marital reconciliation	45
Retirement	45
Change in health of family member	44
Pregnancy	40
Sex difficulties	39
Gain of new family member	39
Business readjustment	39
Change in financial state	38
Death of close friend	37
Change to different line of work	36
Change in number of arguments with spouse	35
Mortgage over $10,000	31
Foreclosure of mortgage or loan	30
Change in responsibilities at work	29
Son or daughter leaving home	29
Trouble with in-laws	29
Outstanding personal achievement	28
Wife begins or stops work	26
Begin or end school	26
Change in living conditions	25
Revision of personal habits	24
Trouble with boss	23
Change in work hours or conditions	20
Change in residence	20
Change in schools	20
Change in recreation	19

Change in church activities 19
Change in social activities 18
Mortgage or loan less than $10,000 17
Change in sleeping habits 16
Change in number of family get-togethers 15
Change in eating habits 15
Vacation 13
Christmas 12
Minor violations of the law .... 11[1]

Many of the events shown on the chart are out of our control. Christmas is going to come every December 25 whether we're ready or not; the death of a spouse, the end of a school year, and restructured work hours often occur without our consent or input. Like it or not, this might be the hand we're dealt. How we choose to play the hand is up to us. Genetically, some of us are better equipped than others to cope with stress. Perhaps we've been blessed with strong bodies, perhaps our relatives have lived long lives, and perhaps there is no history of serious illness in our families. Emotionally, we may be better equipped too. Perhaps we've had happy childhoods that were filled with love and were free of serious conflict. Spiritually, we might have an advantage because we've grown up in the church, have been taught Christian principles, and have been surrounded by godly people who follow these principles. All of these factors are pluses. However, it's important to realize that combating anxiety without them is certainly possible; it's merely more of a challenge.

"It's Your Age"

A poll was once taken among a large group of men, all of whom were older than sixty. What is your greatest regret? was the question posed to each of them. Although their answers varied, several replies surfaced repeatedly: "I didn't listen to the advice of people older and wiser than I was"; "I dropped out of college"; "I didn't stick to anything"; "I played it too safe rather than take a risk"; "I didn't work hard enough."

Much anxiety is blamed on age. But what age? Each period in life has its unique set of obstacles to overcome. Many senior citizens agonize over mistakes they can't undo. They feel it's too late for them, that life has passed them by. They're forced to cope with several of the top stress producers on the Homes and Rahe chart—death of a spouse, deaths of friends and family members, retirement, and personal illness. It's little wonder that depression is a major problem for the elderly, and that 30 percent of all suicide victims are sixty-five and older. In a society that measures a person's value by success on the job, a retiree suffers from loss of self-esteem when he accepts the inevitable gold watch.

Naomi, in the Book of Ruth, is a good example of how an older woman can suffer the anxiety of aging. She outlived her husband and her sons and was too old to start a new family. She was so depressed that when she returned to her former home and was greeted by friends, she told them to call her Mara, the word for "bitter." Not until her daughter-in-law, Ruth, remarried and had a son did Naomi believe she had a purpose again. She became the baby's nurse and once again felt needed. The child gave her value.

"And may he be to you a restorer of life and a nourisher of your old age," said Naomi's friends as they celebrated the baby's birth and Naomi's rebirth of happiness.[2]

The stress attached to old age has only recently been aired. The anxiety connected to the middle years has been the subject of films, books, and jokes for years. It's been dubbed midlife crisis, and it's no laughing matter. Sociologists call people in the middle-aged group the sandwich generation. These middlers still have responsibility for children at home, yet they have a growing responsibility for their aging parents. They're the filling that holds the family unit together. And sometimes it's a sticky job.

Midlife typically includes a grief reaction over reality. When we're young we fantasize about all the success we're going to achieve and all the good works we're going to accomplish. By the time we reach thirty-five or forty—the more insightful we are, the earlier we will suffer midlife crisis—we begin to realize that we will not reach all our goals. We look at ourselves, our mates, our children, and our friends, and we're disappointed. We see faults and weaknesses. *Is this all there is?* we ask ourselves. Anxiety surfaces and we blame it on our age or on our hormones. The truth is, hormones are greatly overexaggerated as an excuse for anxiety. Our emotional upheaval generally causes the changes in our body's chemistry, not vice versa. Our emotions usually drive our hormones rather than our hormones driving our emotions.

If we're looking for an excuse for our anxiety, age is a good one. Youth, midlife, and old age are all stressful. We can graduate from one age group to another, laying the blame and never seeking the source.

Too many people allow themselves to be victimized by circumstances that accompany their ages. As they "outgrow" the problems of adolescence, they progress to the dilemmas of parenting. From there, they move to the crises of midlife and then assume the burdens of senior citizenship. The problems vary, but their anxious reactions are the same, although they may intensify over the years. The solution to all this pain is identical. If the sufferers would learn to look at their emotions and to deal with their feelings, they would be relieved of their discomfort. The same coping strategies that can help them through adolescence also will see them through the challenges of their adult years. These strategies will make them fit to be tried, whatever the trials may be.

"Give It Time"

Time rarely heals anxiety. In fact, it can make it worse. Mental health disorders are illnesses just as surely as heart disease, diabetes, and pneumonia. If they are not diagnosed and treated promptly, they can become more complicated, more serious, even fatal. The American Psychiatric Association estimates that nearly one of every five Americans suffers from some kind of mental illness that should be treated. Panic, phobic, and other anxiety disorders affect almost nine of every one hundred Americans. Unfortunately, fewer than one-third of these people seek help.

Not only can mental disorders be painful; they can be costly. Latest figures indicate that such illnesses cost some $21 billion annually. (That number actually may be higher since it's difficult to put a price tag on lost productivity, errors made by troubled employees, absenteeism, and physical problems that are caused by emotional difficulties.) More mind boggling are the costs of addictions that may be related to anxiety. About $109 billion is spent each year for substance abuse disorders, and an estimated $18 billion for indirect costs of substance abuse disorders. A major motivation for substance abuse is to kill the pain rather than look at the truth about some hidden motive or emotion. This anxiety is a dominant component in substance abuse. Even if severe anxiety could be healed by time, can its victims and society afford to wait?

Realistically, if a person has been counseled for anxiety, he has no guarantee of freedom from suffering forever. Again, mental disorders are illnesses, and illnesses can recur. Think of it this way: If you've been diagnosed as having a sinus infection and treated with antibiotics, you have no assurance that you won't have a similar infection next year. But you'll know what to do if the symptoms arise; you'll know where to get help and how to help yourself. The same is true of mental health problems.

Several years ago, we counseled a missionary wife who was plagued by the constant concern that people didn't like her. She overcompensated by being supermom and superwife. She was an excellent cook, a gracious hostess, and she worked overtime to gain the approval of her husband and his parishioners. Her fear about being disliked was unfounded, but that didn't lessen her pain. She had been rejected frequently by her parents when she was young, and the resulting insecurity carried over into adulthood.

Through counseling we were able to encourage her to develop several deep friendships with people who would appreciate her and affirm her worth. We worked with her husband and showed him how he could boost her self-image with positive support and honest feedback. Finally, we suggested that she become less preoccupied with herself and, instead, focus her attention on other people. We pointed out that while she had served others in the past, her motivation had been to win their approval. Now we wanted her to serve from the heart.

Our efforts were successful, although they were put to the test two years later when this woman's teenage son experienced a period of rebellion and was arrested for theft. We expected the mother would blame herself and slip into her old "I-am-a-failure" mindset.

Our fears were well-founded; that's exactly what happened. However, her regression didn't last long. All her old anxieties surfaced, but this time she knew how to handle them. She had learned to talk about her fears and to face her feelings. Yes, she was down briefly, but she knew how to get up this time. She wasn't permanently paralyzed, just temporarily stunned.

"Anxiety Is a Sign of Total Failure"

Psychiatry makes some people nervous. They don't understand it, and they link it to self-indulging celebrities who delight talk-show hosts with stories about visits to their therapists. Worse yet, people connect psychiatry with loss of control. Mention the word, and images are conjured up of patients being subdued by men in white coats and scenes from such Hollywood caricatures as *One Flew over the Cuckoo's Nest*.

When we were in medical school in the 1960s, the typical curriculum included only one class in general psychiatry. It's no wonder that when we announced to our classmates that we were going to specialize in psychiatry, several of them responded, "You're not going to be real doctors? That's too bad." Fortunately, today's curriculum reflects the new appreciation of the close relationship between mental and physical health. At least one class in psychiatry is offered to all students each year of medical school.

While the medical community finally is adjusting its thinking on therapy, this "enlightenment" is recent and hasn't soaked into other facets of society: big business, for example. Many large companies look with disdain at employees who have psychiatric counseling. They fear that these employees can't handle pressure, might not be executive material, and possibly will require special, delicate treatment on the job. They view emotional problems as weaknesses and don't realize that everyone suffers emotional difficulties to some extent.

It's normal to be sad, to cry, and to feel anxious. Anxiety can be a positive reaction, a signal that a problem needs to be studied, and an emotion needs to be aired. It's unfortunate that more people don't see anxiety as a wonderful built-in mechanism that prods us to look at ourselves. Anxiety can be a strength. To deny the existence of a problem is the real sign of weakness.

"Blame It on Hypoglycemia"

Because many people are uneasy about mental illness, they go to great lengths to explain away symptoms of anxiety and blame the symptoms on physical problems. Since they don't want to admit to being depressed, they attribute their lack of energy to hypoglycemia. Ashamed of their chronic state of jitters, they claim a sluggish thyroid gland. True, hypoglycemia exists, and so does hypothyroidism, but such conditions are rare in comparison to emotional disorders with similar symptoms.

Emotional problems can cause physical illnesses, and physical maladies can lead to emotional disorders. For example, anxiety is at the bottom of such psychophysiological complaints as ulcers, colitis, and migraine headaches. A high percentage of all Americans suffer from headaches, and they are caused overwhelmingly by anxiety. The anxiety is merely displaced to a weak point in the body. Too often the physician treats the symptom and not the source of the trouble. Heavy sedation is prescribed, and the patient is immobilized until the pain subsides. The cycle can go on for years.

Misdiagnosis is especially prevalent among older people. Among senior citizens who are diagnosed as being senile, nearly one of four is actually suffering from a mental illness that could be treated effectively if it were correctly identified. Too often assumptions are made based on symptoms, age, and stereotypes.

By the same token, genuine physical problems can give rise to reactions that appear to be caused by emotional disorders. A patient who has an overactive thyroid gland could easily blame his discomfort on nervousness and continue to suffer for years. The symptoms—perspiration, weight loss, depression—are the same, but the treatments are totally different.

Extensive diagnostic tests are essential to isolate and identify true causes of all illnesses. Some patients are so reluctant to accept a diagnosis of an emotional disorder that they will go from one doctor to another in search of answers they find more favorable.

They prefer that a physical problem be the culprit, and they won't stop until they find a doctor who agrees. Somehow the diagnosis of hypothyroidism or hypoglycemia is easier to accept and to explain to others. The only problem is that with such a diagnosis, the problem never goes away.

"It's a Sin to Dig Up the Past"

We've all known people who live in the past and who hold onto a grudge too long. "Put it behind you," we advise. Then we unleash a series of platitudes: "Let sleeping dogs lie! Forgive and forget. Get on with your life," we urge.

Is it a sin to rehash the past? Yes, if your purpose is to maintain a constant state of anger toward someone. Yes, if in the course of an argument you insist on using a past mistake to belittle the "guilty" party.

However, we all need to dig up the past long enough to identify a long-buried source of current anxiety, to forgive that source as God has taught us to forgive, and then to press on toward the future. There is a strong element of truth attached to the words, "forgive and forget," for we never truly forget until we have truly forgiven. The difficult part, from a psychiatrist's viewpoint, is that the source of anxiety may be so well hidden that the patient isn't consciously aware of its presence. Yet it causes the worry and discomfort that have brought the patient into treatment. The counselor or doctor must search and dig and pump until the memory can be brought to the surface and dealt with. A major issue in dealing with anxiety and unresolved anger is the choice to forgive. Like happiness, forgiveness is a choice.

A good illustration of this is Pat, a young woman who once came to our clinic for treatment of severe panic attacks. She told us during her first counseling session that she and her husband were in the process of getting a divorce. On the surface, the trauma of separation seemed to be a valid reason for her attacks, but she assured us that she wanted the divorce, that the marriage had been unhappy for several years, and that she was looking forward to returning to school.

"So why the panic attacks?" she asked us, genuinely confused.

Several hours of therapy were needed before we could answer her question. We had to go back to her childhood and probe the moment that she learned her father was leaving her mother. In a rush of tears she recalled her father's walking toward the door as she begged him, "Please don't go! Don't leave us. . . ." He had left in spite of her protests, and she had carried a feeling of rejection for years. She was eight years old when the trauma occurred, and on the surface she had recovered nicely from it. However, all the pain returned when she and her husband decided to divorce. Again, she felt rejected by the dominant man in her life. The loss of her husband didn't grieve her as much as the loss of her self-esteem. Would she always be a failure in close relationships? Would she always be rejected by those who knew her best? Would God ultimately reject her too?

Pat's healing came by studying scriptural assurances that God would never reject her, leave her, or stop loving her.[3] Digging up the past enabled her to forgive her father and then to put the painful incident aside. There was no link between her father's leaving his family and the breakup of her marriage. With that knowledge, she was freed of her panic attacks and was free to move on with her future.

"The Devil Made You Do It"

As Christians, we believe demons are involved in all our lives and that Satan is pleased when we suffer the problems of mental disorders. The devil knows where each of us is vulnerable, and he delights in aiming at our weaknesses. Even so, as psychiatrists, we think it's dangerous for troubled patients to believe that someone can cure their problems in an instant without dealing with the deep-seated emotional issues.

If only it were that simple.

We endorse a three-pronged offensive against anxiety. We teach patients to strengthen themselves physically, mentally, and spiritually, based on Paul's prayer for wholeness in "spirit, soul, and body" (1 Thess. 5:23). For example, in the spiritual realm, we like the passage from Ephesians that urges all of us to "put on the whole armor of God, that you may be able to stand against the wiles of the devil."[4] We believe Satan, or the devil, to be a real and mighty opponent. However, overemphasizing demons to the exclusion of personal responsibility or medical resources is an error.

Blaming demons is an easy out. It relieves sufferers of the cause and the cure of their problems. They're not at fault for the affliction, and they have no responsibility in ridding themselves of it. The devil did it.

We believe this kind of thinking is at odds with the Bible's teaching. Jesus continually tells us not to be anxious. Six times in Matthew 6:25–34 the Lord uses the word *worry* as He urges us not to be nervous.[5] This is the proof that we *are* responsible for ridding ourselves of worry. God never commands us to do anything that we are not capable of doing, or that He has not provided enablement to do. By saying we need not worry, He leaves us with a choice. We are not powerless against demons or against the devil.

"Christians Don't Get Nervous"

Of course they do.

Ideally, Christians shouldn't suffer depression, should never become angry, shouldn't be tempted into sin, shouldn't be guilty of materialism, and shouldn't be drawn into power struggles. But Christians are not perfect; we still have the capacity to imitate Adam and to do wrong. We're merely forgiven people who have the resources to deal with our problems and to grow from our experiences.

Evidence of mental disorders among Christians can be found in our clinic's files. Our caseload is about ten thousand a year, and the majority of these patients are Christians. They are good people who have stepped forward and have admitted that yes, they are depressed; yes, they are anxious; and, yes, they even have substance abuse problems. Many of our patients are pastors who for years have denied their burnout, stress, and perfectionism. They're ashamed of the anger they feel toward members of their church who make unrealistic demands on their time, don't support their programs, don't attend their sermons, and cut the church's budget while expanding its outreach. These pastors want to learn to forgive.

Reluctance to see a counselor is based on two beliefs. First, some Christians have been taught that it's a sin to look at themselves. "Look only at Jesus," they've been told. In reality, several scriptural verses suggest that each of us should frequently look at himself. How else can we see our shortcomings? As Christians, our most important goal in life is to become more like Jesus. We do this in two ways: we spend a great deal of time studying Him and a certain amount of time studying ourselves to see how we measure up to Him. Dwight Moody once said that the best way to show that a stick is crooked is not to argue about it or spend time denouncing it, but to lay a straight stick alongside of it. Jesus is our straight stick.

By looking at ourselves and learning about ourselves, we're also able to predict if we are the kinds of persons who are prone to worry. In chapter 4 we'll look at personality types that are apt to be anxious. This self-study is essential to the healing process because if you can predict whether or not you're a prime candidate for worry, than you can prevent the worry from occurring. We'll show you how.

A second reason Christians avoid counseling is that they believe anxiety is a sign of weak faith. If their belief in God were stronger, they say, they wouldn't feel nervous. They would trust the Lord, and their discomfort would go away. For this reason, they avoid all references to worry, depression, anxiety, and other disorders. They find terms that are more compatible with their view of Christianity. They're "under the weather"; their feelings are hurt; and their "feathers are ruffled."

We generally respond to this argument by explaining that weak faith is often a factor, but none of us is perfect. In fact, Scripture exhorts us to admit our faults to one another, encourage one another, and "pray for one another."[6]

Other Christians say that if they just had Jesus Christ present with them to control the physical circumstances surrounding them, they'd suffer from a lot less fear and anxiety and would have a lot more peace and faith. It's unlikely that this would be the case. Scriptures tell us differently.

Toward the end of Jesus' three-year ministry, He and His disciples crossed the lake of Galilee during a severe windstorm. The waves beat against the boat and filled it with water. In spite of the desperate situation, Jesus continued to sleep in the rear of the boat. Finally, the disciples awakened Him.

"Teacher, do You not care that we are perishing?" they asked.

Jesus stood up, halted the raging wind, and told the sea to be still. There was instant calm.

"Why are you so fearful?" He asked His disciples. "How is it that you have no faith?"[7]

The disciples were unable to answer his question. They were in the company of the Son of God, the Savior of man. They had witnessed His miracles daily. Still they were anxious and fearful. They lacked faith. Why? Because they, like us, were only human.

4.

Who's Apt to Be Anxious?

INSECURITY DRIVES PEOPLE to the top. Think about it. The more insecure we are, the more we strive for attention, fame, and success. We're motivated by the need to be noticed. The more secure we are, the less we try to impress. We like us just the way we are.

Psychiatrist Roy Grinker proved this several years ago when he conducted his normality studies in Chicago. His research uncovered an interesting link between anxiety and achievement. He found that the least anxious people were those who had graduated from high school with C+ averages, had bypassed college in favor of factory jobs, tended to be religious, spent a good deal of time with their wives and two children, and generally enjoyed who they were and what they had. They were satisfied with life in a split-level, and their aspirations were no more ambitious than buying a SuperSaver to DisneyWorld and a new station wagon every four years. They liked being average.[1]

High achievers were different. Not only were they less satisfied, but they were more anxious. Many of them were insecure because they had grown up in a conditional "we'll-love-you-if . . ." kind of environment. Rather than having parents who loved them no matter what they accomplished, they had to work to earn Mom and Dad's affection. "We'll love you *if* you make perfect (or nearly perfect) grades," their parents said. "We'll be proud of you *if* you earn a varsity letter." Love was a reward for performance. It was measured in degrees and was directly related to the level of success that was attained.

Push. Win. Excel. Before long, competition can become a way of life. Patterns are established, and personalities are shaped. On the surface, these personalities are labeled as "winners." Underneath, they often struggle for survival. Take Peter M., for example.

Two Cheers for the Winner

Dr. Peter M. had always been driven, first by his mother and father, and then by himself. He was the oldest son of hard-working, perfectionistic parents. No matter what he did in his early years, it always fell short of pleasing them. He couldn't be potty-trained soon enough; he couldn't make the transition from bottle to cup early enough; he couldn't learn to read fast enough to suit them. Although he earned straight A's throughout elementary, middle, and high school, he endured criticism if an occasional paper was less than perfect.

Like most children, Peter looked up to his parents and assumed they were correct in their expectations of him. He grew up believing he was inferior for not being good enough to please them. And that made him try all the harder. He pushed, he worked, and he excelled. He graduated from college summa cum laude and was accepted into medical school where he maintained his top-of-the-class ranking. Personally and professionally he oozed confidence and success. No one was aware of the tension that plagued him constantly.

"I've always known I was a workaholic, but I never thought I was suicidal," he said, after signing himself into our hospital treatment center in suburban Dallas. He was frightened. The depression he had suffered for years had become so severe that he had purchased a small handgun with the intention of taking his life. Therapy was never considered as an option. He viewed the need for counseling as a sign of weakness. *Why admit to the world that you can't solve your own problems?* was his attitude. Not until he had lost control and had put the gun to his head one day did he realize the seriousness of his emotional disorder. *What am I doing?* his rational side screamed at him. He stopped short of pulling the trigger and reached out for help just in time.

Peter's was a tough case to solve. Because of his education, intelligence, and perfectionistic nature, he was able to dodge the truth with sophisticated defense mechanisms. He was a brilliant doctor who understood our diagnoses and could counter them with logical alternatives. On the surface he seemed eager to be cured, but subconsciously he resisted treatment and cleverly worked to keep his feelings hidden. Another man with far less education than Peter checked into the hospital on the same day. He was well within three weeks. Peter's therapy required four months of hospitalization and numerous outpatient counseling sessions.

Before we could probe the problems that Peter denied, we concentrated on the one he acknowledged: workaholism. He admitted that he loved his wife and children, but he felt guilty spending too much leisure time with them. *Get back to work,* his subconscious always nagged.

We pointed out that he was a workaholic for three reasons:

- For years his parents had demanded perfection from him, and the only way he could be assured of delivering a flawless performance was to work constantly at it.
- Whenever he looked around for role models, his eyes settled on the people closest to him—his mother and father—and they were always working.
- By putting in long, exhausting hours he was too busy and too tired to examine the pain, hurt, and anger that he felt toward his parents.

The third reason was the key. If he ever was to be free of his anxiety, he had to face the truth that he had denied all his life. He had to admit that he resented his mother and father for the impossible demands they had placed on him. He was furious at himself for the years he had cooperated in their "we'll-love-you-if . . ." games. They had issued the challenges, and he had immersed himself in striving to meet them. He had failed every time, but had been kept in a type of bondage by the possibility of success.

Not only did Peter have to admit his anger, he also had to take his parents off their pedestal. They weren't perfect; they had flaws; they were human too. Next, he had to abandon all hope that they would ever accept him unconditionally. He would never be quite good enough in their eyes. He needed to forfeit all their "we'll-love-you-if . . ." games because he couldn't win. Finally, he had to rebuild his self-image. The fact that he couldn't please two of the 5.1 billion people who inhabit the earth didn't mean that he had no value.

Peter wasn't a Christian when he entered the hospital, but he was willing to listen as we shared God's plan of salvation. We assured him that with God, salvation comes not by work but by grace. Unlike his parents, God puts no conditions on love. It's not a matter of "I'll love you *if . . .*" but rather "I'll love you *no matter what.*" Together we read Ephesians 2:8–9: "For by grace you have been saved through faith, and that not of yourselves; it is the gift of God, not of works, lest anyone should boast."

Peter's progress was slow. For years he had tried to be invincible; now we were telling him to be vulnerable. Since he was a child he had been taught to keep his emotions in check; now we were urging him to release those feelings and laugh, cry, and be angry. We were even trying to accomplish the unthinkable: reduce his parents to human status, complete with shortcomings and flaws. In addition, we were asking him to accept and forgive these flaws and to love his parents unconditionally—something they would never be able to do in return.

"We should always honor our parents and respect them," we told Peter. "But we have to realize that no one is perfect. Just as we should forgive our parents for their imperfections, we should also ask our children to forgive us for ours."

We explained that many of the mistakes we make with our children are the same mistakes our parents made with us. History repeats itself, and so do errors. When a child says he's angry, we often convince him that he isn't. He believes us and denies his anger. When he cries, we tell him "big boys don't cry," and we offer a reward if he'll stop. He feels guilty for not measuring up to "big boy" status, covers his pain, and accepts his prize. In both instances, the feelings don't go away, but are merely hidden. In varying degrees we parents teach our children to lie about emotions.

Through therapy, Peter finally was able to look at his true feelings. His anger toward his parents and toward himself was replaced with forgiveness. He realized he couldn't base his self-worth on his parents' assessment. He was a child of God and would base his self-worth on God's unconditional love. He would try not to make the same mistakes with his children that his parents had made with him; but he was human, he was vulnerable, and errors were inevitable. He learned to forgive himself and to ask for forgiveness from others.

By looking back at his past and coming to grips with his long-buried feelings, Peter was able to design an action plan for his future. Changes were in order. He decided to balance his time better and to give top priority to his young family. He curbed his patient load so that his workday didn't spill over into evenings and the week could be contained within Monday-through-Friday parameters. He knew that his career as a surgeon would always be packed with pressure and that he would always demand excellence of himself in his work. The difference was that now he took an inner peace into the turmoil of his profession.

Type A Personality

Peter has what psychiatrists call an obsessive-compulsive personality. In trendier terms, his personality bears the Type A label. Many high achievers are Type A, and most of them boast about the traits that are linked with the type. It's easy to see why. Type A people are intelligent perfectionists who have a tendency toward being obstinate. They're dedicated workers, seldom overlook details, and are as neat in their appearance as they are in their work. Almost like the legendary Mr. Spock of *Star Trek,* they prefer facts to feelings. They're logical and make excellent problem solvers. But they're feisty too. They enjoy playing devil's advocate, and for the sake of argument they'll often take the opposing point of view on any topic and build a good case. They love to win (and generally do), but the real sport is scoring the points. Flexibility may not be their strength, but then, nobody's perfect. However, they never stop trying.

Obsessive-compulsive people are as marked for anxiety as they are for success. No one is more apt to be anxious than a Type A person. The same traits that cause him to excel also cause him to worry. He sets high goals and works tirelessly to reach them. If he falls short, he's devastated. He has no patience with failure or mediocrity. Not only does he expect perfection of himself but also of everyone around him. With unrealistic expectations such as these, he endures a lot of disappointment. Frequent disappointment leads to more anxiety, and the cycle begins again.

The Type A person usually chooses a challenging career that requires a great deal of training. Even after he completes his education and enters his field, he is under constant stress. That's the nature of his job—whatever it is—and that's one reason he chose it. It's not surprising that more than 90 percent of the doctors and 76 percent of the pastors we have tested show strong Type A personality traits.[2]

Women are just as likely to be obsessive-compulsive as men. Their tendency toward perfectionism and workaholism has always been there, but it generally went unnoticed until recent years when women became a more potent force in the business world. Still, one of the best illustrations of a Type A person that we have is a woman of biblical days.

Martha, like most obsessive-compulsive workaholics, lived in the future. She loved to plan and prepare, but she didn't know how to relax and enjoy. She welcomed Jesus and his disciples into her home but then spent most of the time fretting over dinner. She expected her sister, Mary, to help her and was disappointed when Mary decided to relax and enjoy their guests. Rather than sitting at Jesus' feet to hear his teaching, Martha chose to work. She expected to be praised for her efforts, but instead, Jesus gently pointed out that she was too concerned with details and that Mary had made the wiser choice to sit and listen.

"There is really only one thing worth being concerned about," said Jesus. "Mary has discovered it."[3]

Though separated by centuries, Martha and Dr. Peter M. share characteristics. Both were consumed by their work and were driven to achieve. They felt guilty about relaxing, and they craved compliments. Peter needed the approval of his parents, and Martha sought the praise of Jesus. "Will you love me if I become a rich and famous surgeon?" Peter subconsciously asked his parents. Martha seemed to say to Jesus, "Will you be impressed with me if my house is in perfect order and I serve you a delicious meal?" Because they misinterpreted negative answers to mean that their performances had fallen short, their only recourse was to work even harder.

"A" Pluses and Minuses

Obsessive-compulsive people have a lot going for them—and a lot working against them. Although they tend to see every issue as right or wrong, black or white, their Type A character traits are a mixed bag. Some are good, some are bad. Color them gray.

Ten descriptive traits of a Type A person are:

1. He is extremely moral.
2. Although torn between rebellion and obedience, he generally chooses obedience.
3. His appearance is neat and clean.
4. Organization is one of his strengths.
5. He is an outstanding student.
6. He is conscientious.
7. He is very punctual.
8. He has a heightened power of concentration.
9. He performs well on the job.
10. He enjoys competition.

All of these traits are positive. No one would object to being described as a moral, well-organized, conscientious worker. But there's a flip side. We might call these the "A" minuses.

Ten equally accurate ways of summing up an obsessive-compulsive person are:

1. He is stubborn.
2. He worries constantly.
3. He cannot relax.
4. He is insecure.
5. He can't tolerate criticism, but he's critical of others.
6. He adheres to strict rules as a way of covering his uncertainty.
7. He refuses to assume blame for his mistakes.
8. He wants to be perceived as being perfect.
9. He is stingy with money, love, and time.

10. Secretly he often questions his own salvation.[4]

While the first list of traits suggests success, the second assures anxiety. Unfortunately, today's society encourages and rewards perfectionism and workaholic behavior. In part, this is why anxiety currently is the number one mental health disorder. Life in the 1980s zooms by at a fast-forward pace. In medicine nearly 50 percent of all medical knowledge is outdated every five years. The pressure is on to keep up with the changes and ahead of the pack. There are books to consume, journals to study, lectures to attend.

In business, living in the future is in vogue; the practice of viewing life in one-year and five-year blocks (labeled short-term objectives and long-range goals) is the management style that everyone champions. As soon as one set of goals is reached, the next set is adopted. The idea is never to have a final destination, but always to be in transit. On the surface, this constant motion agrees with Type A persons. Since their natural bent is to push hard, they enjoy a system that rewards players who put forth the best effort. The unhappy byproduct is that many young executives are developing hypertension, ulcers, and other physical disorders as well as burnout and the emotional and spiritual complications that accompany life in the fast lane.[5]

Even if the obsessive-compulsive person can control his perfectionism to make it work in his favor on the job, he can suffer its effects on the home front. There, his rigid point of view doesn't change, only the scenario. He still sees everything in black and white, wrong and right terms. If he falters and makes a mistake, he can't bear the guilt. If he slips into an extramarital affair, for instance, he often develops overwhelming anxiety. He gives up on himself, believes he is beyond redemption, and moves to the other extreme. He resigns himself to a sinful life.

The Birth-Order Factor

What do George Washington, Gloria Steinem, Henry Ford, and Abraham have in common? Beyond being high achievers in their time and among their peers, they share another characteristic: Each was the first-born child in his family.

If Type A personalities are the most apt to be anxious, first-born children are the most likely to be Type A. Research has proven that birth order has an impact on personality development and therefore on the amount of anxiety that individuals will endure. Of course, personality development and anxiety are both influenced by several factors. The birth order is the one we are emphasizing in this chapter. Our staff at the Minirth-Meier Clinic knows this first-hand because a high percentage of the patients we treat for anxiety disorders are the oldest children in their families and have obsessive-compulsive personalities.

What about the others? Middle children often handle anxiety best because they're survivors. They've learned how to be heard above the din of the crowd, they know how to communicate their needs to their parents, and they're seasoned diplomats when it comes to interacting with their older and younger brothers and sisters. The youngest child, on the other hand, sometimes has problems with anxiety because he is used to being dependent. Mother often holds on to her youngest longer, and the little one likes to lean on Mom. When the prop is removed, he looks for another. Sometimes the support he finds has negative value, such as drugs, alcohol, or codependent relationships.

"First-born children . . . tend to be more conscientious, achieve higher scholastically, and go to school longer than later-borns," says Dr. Lucille Forer. "They also are more apt to become scientists or eminent in their chosen careers than are later children in the family. But the first-born also may be jealous and angrier than a middle or youngest brother or sister. He may be tense and driven because of parents who no longer provided exclusive attention after the next baby was born. Parents also expect a higher level of achievement from their first child than from later children."[6]

Oldest children are high-risk candidates for anxiety for five reasons. First, their parents are new to parenting and don't know what to expect. So they expect too much. Mom and Dad usually learn to relax when number two comes along, but for now they rivet their eyes on their first-born and watch for reasons to boast. Baby feels the pressure to deliver.

Second, unless the first-born is an only child, he eventually must endure the trauma of little brother's (or sister's) arrival. This puts him in a highly competitive situation. The newcomer has the spotlight and everyone's attention. The first-born has to work harder to lure the eyes that once were focused on him.

Third, the first-born has no big brother or big sister to look up to as a role model. He only has Mom and Dad. If they show a tendency toward workaholism and perfectionism, he takes his cue from them. Like father, like son; like mother, like daughter. Since 85 percent of an adult's personality is formed by the time he is six years old, his later, more relaxed role models—friends, teachers, and neighbors—are going to have only a secondary impact.

Fourth, many first-born children today are expected to assume surrogate mother or father roles in single-parent homes. The parents are divorced, the mother has custody of the children, and the first-born is given the responsibility of disciplining brothers and sisters while Mom is at work. Anxiety results when a youngster is expected to juggle the roles of child and adult simultaneously. He's playing teacher while he's still a student. His immature emotions buckle under his adult duties. Pressure results.

Finally, because of their naturally competitive nature and their discomfort at sharing feelings, first-born children sometimes don't make friends easily. As "loners," they don't talk through their problems, but keep concerns to themselves. Emotions aren't ventilated, and worries aren't put in perspective by friendly sounding boards. Instead, anxiety builds. Classmates are viewed not as confidantes but as rivals for grades, honors, and leadership positions.

Don't Downgrade the Upside

Generalizations are just as easy to refute as they are to defend. Not all first-born children have obsessive-compulsive personalities, and not all Type A people suffer high anxiety. Neither is all anxiety bad. In chapter 5 we'll explore the fine line between positive and negative anxiety and show you how to determine which type you are experiencing, how to channel it if it's positive, and how to correct it if it's negative.

At our clinic we've treated anxiety disorders in patients with personality types other than obsessive-compulsive, and people in different birth-order positions. Statistics merely advise us of trends, and the trends indicate that first-borns are prone to Type A personalities, and Type A personalities are prone to anxiety.

Don't be alarmed if you diagnose yourself as Type A. We and many of our staff members admit to an abundance of obsessive-compulsive personality traits and probably couldn't have completed medical school and seminary training without them. Being competitive, disciplined, and punctual has value, especially in classroom and professional settings. In spite of our Type A traits, we enjoy rewarding careers and relaxing personal lives. You can too. It just takes a little work to work a little less.

Recognizing a tendency toward perfectionism and workaholism is helpful in controlling work habits and keeping negative anxiety to a minimum. We doctors carefully monitor not only our own schedules and anxiety levels, but those of our coworkers as well. Recently the executive director of our clinic was diagnosed as having "running pneumonia." This is a stepped-up version of walking pneumonia and seemed appropriate since he had a habit of running through airports, O. J. Simpson style. Because of his Type A personality, he insisted on keeping all his appointments including seminars, speaking engagements, and administrative responsibilities. As his friends, we finally stepped in, encouraged him to cancel his obligations, and sent him home to bed. He objected, but we overruled. Doctors' orders. He survived both the pneumonia *and* the brief sabbatical.

5.

Over the Brink

ANXIETY CAN BE positive or negative, healthy or unhealthy. Tuning in to know which is which sometimes requires a trained eye and an expert ear. In some ways a psychiatrist is like Sherlock Holmes. He has to be a good detective who asks a lot of questions, looks for clues, collects pieces of the puzzle, and tries to put them together into a picture he can understand and evaluate. As we saw in chapter 4, some of these clues may relate to birth order and personality traits. But no matter how experienced the psychiatrist is and regardless of how obvious the clues seem, occasionally he pursues "blind leads" and comes up empty-handed.

Which reminds us of Marilyn G.

When Marilyn's concerned family admitted her to our Texas hospital unit, she was delusional and was slipping in and out of reality. We were faced with two challenges: First, we had to restore the chemical balance in her brain so that she would leave her fantasy world and be able to benefit from therapy; second, we had to do our detective work and find out what was causing her intense, abnormal anxiety. To accomplish this we not only had to spend a great deal of time asking Marilyn questions, but we also had to interview her family. We needed to know as precisely as possible when Marilyn had begun acting irrationally. Then we had to determine what might have triggered her increased stress.

But first things first.

Marilyn was schizophrenic. Confused, she rambled incoherently, drifted into a private world that no one else could enter, and sat for long periods of time staring into space showing no expression or emotion. Although schizophrenic disorders sometimes are depicted in films and on television as being common and humorous

63

(the man who thinks he's Napoleon), they are neither. They affect only about 1 percent of the adult population, and they can cause permanent damage to the untreated patient.

We knew that the extreme anxiety Marilyn had suffered for several weeks probably had caused an imbalance in her level of dopamine, a neurotransmitter in the brain. In simple terms, here's what often happens in cases like Marilyn's: A patient under stress experiences an increased flow of body chemicals. A certain amount of this can reap positive results. For instance, a public speaker sometimes will comment that his "adrenalin is flowing" right before he takes the microphone. He feels hyped up, alert, and anxious in a positive sense. But if this stepped-up, nervous state continues for a prolonged period, the positive aspects become negative. The body tires; some chemical levels are depleted, while others remain abnormally high. All this contributes to an imbalance that can bring on mood swings, depression, euphoria, and even maybe one factor in schizophrenia.

If, for example, the chemical norepinephrine dips to a low ebb, depression is likely to occur. When dopamine levels go too high, as they did in Marilyn, schizophrenic behavior can surface. Fortunately, drugs known as major tranquilizers were introduced in the 1950s and can play a vital part in treating this kind of disorder. Success rates vary from patient to patient, of course, and timing is important: the sooner the better.

Marilyn responded well to our prescribed drug treatment. With her fragile chemical balance reinstated, she was ready for therapy. Then the tough part began.

In talking with her family, we determined that Marilyn's anxiety first was noticed after an unfortunate event occurred with her eight-year-old daughter, Heidi, and an elderly neighbor. Because the gentleman was ninety, senile, and very frail, he rarely left his son's home unaccompanied. However, one afternoon he was out for a walk when Heidi passed on her way from school. The old man reached out and grabbed the child and fondled her. Heidi easily freed herself, ran home, and told her mother.

A normal reaction would have been for Marilyn to feel angry

at the man and anxious about the incident's effect on Heidi. The anger might have prompted her to telephone the man's son, tell him what had happened, and urge him not to allow the old man to wander the neighborhood alone. Her anxiety might have caused her to discuss the event with Heidi, determine if the child seemed overly troubled by it, and if so, schedule a visit to a counselor to help the little girl ventilate her feelings. Such anger and anxiety on Marilyn's part would have been normal and healthy. This would have been an example of positive anxiety. Instead, she overreacted. She became enraged, cried uncontrollably, and wouldn't let go of her wrath.

Often it's a fine line that separates normal anxiety from the abnormal variety. *Much depends on how intense the anxiety is, how long it lasts, what brings it on in the first place, and how frequently it returns.* Positive anxiety is an asset, a built-in alarm system that signals possible danger. In Marilyn's case, it would have led to one-on-one discussions between mother and daughter about senility, sexuality, and safety. Negative anxiety, on the other hand, is an alarm system with its wires crossed—it goes off for the wrong reason (or for no reason at all), at the wrong times, and often can't be silenced. This kind of anxiety isn't a *warning* of danger, but a danger itself.

After hearing the story of Heidi's encounter with the old man, we rightly assumed that Marilyn's disorder was somehow linked to it. Not only did the timing of the events lead us to that conclusion, but whenever we mentioned the elderly man to Marilyn she became visibly agitated. She fidgeted with her handkerchief, red blotches formed on her neck, and her breathing became more rapid.

Our first thought was that Heidi's experience triggered some long-buried memory from Marilyn's childhood. Perhaps she had been sexually abused when she was young, and perhaps she had repressed her anger for all these years. Yes, that made sense; only the pieces of the puzzle didn't fit. When we asked Marilyn if she had suffered a similar incident, she said no, and her denial wasn't accompanied by any telltale symptoms of anxiety. She didn't react with tears, nervous gestures, or other obvious red flags. We concluded that she was telling the truth. Further investigation supported this conclusion. We were assured that she had enjoyed a happy childhood and had been guided by loving parents.

We rejected the theory.

Still, we suspected Marilyn's severe anxiety was somehow sexually linked. Why else would it reveal itself so passionately after Heidi's experience? Why else would she react so visibly whenever she spoke of the incident? We knew her marriage was solid, and now we had determined that her early years had been happy too. We decided to examine several past events in Marilyn's life very cautiously to see their possible effect on the present. We urged Marilyn to talk about a variety of experiences and watched for reactions that would tip us off to the problem. The place to start seemed to be the years between childhood and marriage. We asked about college, and we focused particularly on any intimate relationships she might have had with men during that period. She began to show anxiety when she admitted she had experienced two unwanted pregnancies.

"Both ended with abortions," she explained.

"Any guilt feelings?" we asked.

"No."

If we had merely listened to her words, we might have accepted her denial and rejected that theory as well. But as we listened, we watched. Her words sent one message, but her body language was saying something else. Whenever such mixed messages are received, the observer generally puts more credence in the nonverbal communication. Not only did Marilyn refuse to look at us, but she folded her arms tightly across her chest and crossed her legs away from us. In a not-so-subtle way she was covering up her emotions (folding her arms over her heart) and pulling away (directing her crossed legs toward the door). At the same time, the small red blotches appeared around her collar and the fidgeting began. We knew we were onto something.

"Let's talk about the abortions," we said. "You seem a little defensive about them."

In spite of her constant denials of guilt, we continued to probe the circumstances surrounding the abortions. By asking very specific questions, we caused her to go back to the moment she had learned she was pregnant, made the decision to abort the babies, and endured the procedures that followed. She recalled the counseling sessions when a nurse assured her she was not destroying a life but merely ridding her body of unwanted tissue. As she poured out the details she became noticeably agitated. Deep feelings of shame and grief surfaced. They were ventilated painfully and were accompanied by a deluge of tears.

Intellectually Marilyn had dealt with her early pregnancies when they occurred. She had looked at her choices and had made the one that seemed right at the time. Her decision to abort was history. However, she had never dealt with that decision on an emotional level. Her feelings, repressed for so many years, had never been resolved and were still very much a part of her present being. She wasn't aware of these emotions on a conscious level and might never have faced them if Heidi's experience hadn't stirred them to the point that they were clamoring for attention.

How do you put to rest strong feelings of guilt, sorrow, and regret so many years after they were formed? Marilyn did it symbolically by talking to her unborn babies and apologizing to them for her decision to end their lives. She grieved about their deaths and told them that someday she would join them in heaven. Perhaps most importantly, she forgave herself for the choice she had made so many years ago. She also forgave the people who had counseled her to make that choice. After working through this intense mix of feelings, she finally found peace within herself. She was healed.

Too Much of a Good Thing?

Marilyn's story is extreme. Her anxiety literally was driving her insane. Unfortunately, all psychiatrists have many Marilyns in their files, and some patients aren't able to resolve their problems as successfully as she was. Such cases may represent anxiety over the brink, the negative, harmful variety of worry.

While doctors maintain that anxiety *can* be a good thing, we know that too much of a good thing can be destructive. Perhaps the best illustration of this is in the workplace. Most successful managers realize that employees perform better if they have a realistic concern about their jobs. If they know their jobs, their promotions, and their raises depend on their performance, they're motivated to put forth their best effort. If they feel too secure, they may become careless, lazy, and lax. On the other hand, if they worry too much about being laid off or fired, their productivity may decrease, absenteeism may increase, and quality may suffer. Again, a little anxiety keeps people on their toes, but too much anxiety can cause them to stumble and fall.

Agoraphobia

From time to time a particular type of anxiety disorder captures the media's attention and results in the reading and viewing public's enduring a megadose of information about the over-the-brink anxiety disorder. Most recently this has occurred with agoraphobia, which has been the subject of television documentaries and numerous magazine articles.

Agoraphobia, simply defined, is an overpowering fear of being alone or in some public place where no retreat or escape is possible. It is negative anxiety and has no positive value. To an agoraphobic, the worst scenario would be to find himself in a busy mall or on a crowded city street when he suffers a panic attack, some kind of seizure, or even death. Virtually all persons who develop agoraphobia have experienced at least one panic attack, and the experience has been so terrifying that the memory of it haunts them. Sometimes they avoid the place where the attack occurred, sometimes they avoid all places that slightly resemble the place where the attack occurred, and sometimes just the recollection of the attack is so painful that it brings on another attack. Anxiety can breed anxiety.

About 5 percent of Americans have experienced agoraphobia to some degree.[1] It can come and go, or it can come and stay. In its most severe form it can last a lifetime. Some victims slowly withdraw from society until they become housebound. Since three times as many women as men are afflicted, often the sufferers are overlooked and merely are labeled as "homebodies."

The good news about agoraphobia is that, like all anxiety disorders, it is treatable. Medication is often helpful (antidepressants are prescribed to prevent panic attacks and benzodiazepines can be used temporarily to ease the anxiety caused by anticipation of an attack), and training in relaxation techniques is recommended. Education is also vital. The patient needs to learn that panic attacks aren't nearly as dangerous as they are frightening. Because the symptoms are similar to those of a heart attack—stepped-up breathing, pounding heart, dizziness—the patient often thinks he is dying. Such a fear can make the attack even more intense. It's comforting to know that although the heart rate does increase some forty beats per minute during a panic attack, such an increase is no cause for alarm. The heart rate is not in any kind of danger zone; in fact, it's still slower than the heart rate of a person undergoing a treadmill test or doing aerobic exercises.

Agoraphobia is just one serious anxiety disorder. Dozens of others exist. And schizophrenia, as Marilyn's case illustrates, can produce anxiety symptoms. In their book *Everything You Wanted to Know about Phobias but Were Afraid to Ask,* Dr. Neal Olshan and Julie Wang list more than two hundred documented specific phobias. These range from the common such as claustrophobia (fear of confinement) and acrophobia (fear of heights) to the bizarre such as meteorophobia (fear of meteors) and barophobia (fear of gravity).[2]

Other Phobias

We see examples of phobias and other types of negative anxiety every day. We've treated patients who fear that if they start crying they won't be able to stop or if they ever let their anger surface they might lose control and hurt someone. We've counseled a pastor's wife whose obsession with germs caused her to wash her hands a hundred times a day. Then there was the young man who spent three-fourths of his waking hours making lists because he was so afraid he was going to forget something. Compulsions prompt people to return home several times to make sure the stove is really turned off or the doors are tightly locked. We recall one woman who would drive down the highway and think that she saw a person lying on the side of the road. She would retrace her route over and over again looking for the body that wasn't there. Another patient, a man, worried himself sick that a campfire he once had started in a national park hadn't been properly dowsed.

Cases such as these may seem silly to everyone but the persons who suffer the anxiety of them. This anxiety goes from harmless to serious (over the brink) when three questions are answered with "yes" responses:

• Is your worry preventing you from functioning on the job or at home?
• Is your behavior about to get you into trouble?
• Has this nervousness gone on for several weeks?

The Positive Side of Anxiety

Although excessive anxiety—stemming from phobias, compulsions, schizophrenia—gets the majority of attention, we'd be wrong in not giving equal time to the flip side, the positive side. *Anxiety can be a wonderful emotion if it is temporary and if it leads to responsible behavior.* It can be helpful if it lets you know that something is going on in your private world that needs to be studied and dealt with.

For examples of positive anxiety we look at our own lives. At different points in our pasts we doctors have been nudged by anxiety to take directions we might not otherwise have taken. You could say that when it comes to discussing positive anxiety, we speak from experience.

Fit for a Long Fight

Dr. Minirth's life-changing encounter with anxiety occurred when he was twelve and was diagnosed as having diabetes mellitus. Even at that young age he was a serious student and generally turned to books to learn about topics he didn't understand. The information he found on diabetes was not encouraging. He read that it could be debilitating, slowly taking its toll on its victims. Often the kidneys are weakened; sometimes the eyes are affected until blindness occurs. Not only would he have to endure daily injections but he would have to avoid many of the foods teenagers crave. His life would have to be extremely well disciplined if he was to enjoy any degree of normalcy. Whether he liked it or not, the disease that would burden him for the rest of his life was going to make him different.

It's easy to imagine his anxiety as he realized that at any time his blood sugar level could shoot up and leave him comatose. This happened just three years after the diagnosis when a serious bout with pneumonia was complicated by the diabetes and he was hospitalized. The attending physicians were grim in their outlook for the thin, frail boy, but Frank surprised them. He fought hard and was home within a week. Two weeks later he was back at school.

If you were to ask Frank Minirth today how he managed to withstand the mental and physical rigors of college and medical school and emerge healthier than ever in spite of his ever-present diabetes, he would claim anxiety as one of his motivators. Long before most youngsters become concerned with diet and fitness, Frank was being briefed by his doctors on all the negative possibilities connected to lifestyle and his disease. Taking good care of himself wasn't just advisable; it was essential. He made an early decision not to become weak and vulnerable, because he knew that such poor physical condition would make him prey to the disease's side effects. He designed a plan to build up his body so it could sustain setbacks. He jogged, lifted weights, and followed a program similar to the one outlined in chapters 5 and 10. He gained weight, grew taller, and developed his muscles. Prodded by concern for his future, he made himself fit for the long fight.

His diabetes had at least two other positive effects on his life. Since his condition had to be constantly monitored by doctors, he became interested in medicine as a profession. Later, in college, he met Mary Alice, his future bride. One of the qualities that attracted Mary Alice to Frank was his dogged determination to beat the odds of his disease and to succeed in his special medical ministry. She admired the way his healthy anxiety about what *could* happen motivated him to make sure that it didn't.

"Work for the Night Is Coming"

Dr. Meier's anxiety, like Dr. Minirth's, began as a healthy

motivator. He had always been a good student, but he knew that good wasn't good enough if he hoped to achieve his career goal of becoming a psychiatrist. In the competitive pre-med program at Michigan State only the very best progressed to medical school. Paul was *anxious* to excel. Even after he established himself as a straight-A student he wasn't satisfied. He was determined to do well in other aspects of life. As he recalls in *The Workaholic and His Family:*

> One year in college, I carried thirty-nine hours in two semesters, played two sports, worked nights as a private nurse for an elderly evangelist with organic brain syndrome, was the president of two campus organizations, spent over an hour a day in personal devotions, read a book a week in addition to my studies, did charitable work on weekends, got engaged to be married, and won an award at the end of the school year for having achieved a straight-A record. Needless to say, I was a first-class workaholic, and I was proud of myself for being one.[3]

Such a frenzied pace, born out of genuine concern, may have been positive at the outset but became negative as the heavy workload evolved into a way of life. Anything short of an eighteen-hour day seemed lax to Paul as he began his medical career. Fortunately, anxiety stepped in to cause Paul to put on the brakes and stop the skid that was pulling him away from his family. One morning as he meditated on Scripture during his regular 5:00 A.M. devotional time, he was struck by the irony of the passage he was reading: "My yoke is easy and My burden is light."[4]

Easy? Light? It seemed exactly the opposite to him. He realized that he felt weighted down by his efforts to be all things to all people. Even his commitment to Christ wasn't a source of joy but was another obligation that tugged on him. He was pulled in so many directions that he worried constantly that he might fall short, not get a job done correctly, or disappoint someone. This moment of truth, characterized by a burst of anxiety, caused him to stop and scrutinize his life. Not liking what he saw, he immediately outlined a plan of change. But the change required more than two years to implement fully.

Sometimes freedom from one kind of anxiety only sets off another kind. When Paul cleared some clutter from his calendar, he found himself faced with guilt, which is an anxiety-producing problem all its own. He felt guilty about saying no to persons who asked him to serve on worthwhile committees, to friends who needed his counsel away from the office, and to community groups that invited him to speak to them. He also experienced hostility from people in his church who had come to depend on his time and talents for their good works. They wondered why he was suddenly being so selfish and opting for family activities rather than pitching in and helping their ministry. Finally, he had to deal with several painful insights that he never had time for when he was racing from one obligation to another. Without dozens of extra concerns on his mind, he had quiet moments to examine his shortcomings and insecurities. He realized he had enough problems of his own to solve, and it was time for him to concentrate on them.

Burning the Candle at Both Ends

Author Don Hawkins easily relates to Dr. Meier's experience. As senior pastor of a large midwestern church for several years, Don directed a multifaceted ministry. In addition to his responsibilities at the church, he managed a Christian radio station and was a professor of communications at a Christian college. Each of these activities constituted a full-time occupation. Despite his relatively high level of energy, Don soon found himself burning out. Since he was committed to spending time with his family, he often deprived himself of valued rest. In fact, he averaged about four hours of sleep per night and got up at 4:15 each morning to be on the air by 6:00 A.M. A key part of Don's problem involved anxiety about being available to minister to people, coupled with a need to look at his underlying workaholism.

It was during this frenetic time in his life that his caring friends and family pointed out that no one can burn the candle at both ends without ultimately burning out. Don realized that if he were to survive for the long haul, he had better live life one day at a time.

He made many difficult adjustments. He first looked at the

truth and recognized that other people could share in the demands of his ministry. Other persons could host the morning segment of programming on the radio station, and others could take care of certain administrative responsibilities at the church. Don changed his schedule, gave up the early morning hours and some of the late evening commitments, and became less and less worried that he might not get a job done correctly or might disappoint someone who expected him to be available or to do a certain task.

Anxiety as a Tool

The anxiety Marilyn G. suffered and that Frank Minirth, Paul Meier, and Don Hawkins experienced are light years apart. Anxiety's spectrum is broad.

In this chapter we've described anxiety as a negative condition that can cause pain and lead to serious mental illness. We've also likened it to an alarm system that can grab your attention and sound the warning of potential danger. Living a worry-free life involves learning to identify anxiety quickly, which involves four steps:

- You need to become familiar with how anxiety usually presents itself in you. Is it sleeplessness? Headaches? Hives? Excessive perspiration?
- As in Marilyn's case, you should note exactly when the symptoms of anxiety first become obvious.
- Knowing at what point your anxiety was touched off, search yourself for its source. Ask yourself: Am I angry with someone? Did someone hurt my feelings? Am I experiencing guilt for something I said or did?
- Finally, ventilate your feelings and make amends. Talk out your anger or hurt with the other person who was involved. Apologize if you were at fault, and forgive him if he was to blame.

Just as surely as our bodies were designed by God, they were equipped with a built-in diagnostic and maintenance tool called anxiety. Think of it this way: When a red light flashes on your car's dashboard, you know you have a potential problem, and you know that as a responsible driver you need to pull off the road, lift the hood, isolate the problem, and fix it. Anxiety serves you in the same way. When it grabs your attention, you need to pull out of the fast lane, look deeply within, seek the source, and fix the problem. Part of this repair process involves becoming aware of tricky coverups we call defense mechanisms. In the next chapter we'll show you how to recognize them and how to strip away the layers of deceit so that you can clearly see and deal with the truth they hide.

6.

The Coverups: Defense Mechanisms

WHEN AMERICA'S FIRST superhero, Superman, arrived on the scene from Cleveland, not Krypton, in 1938, he saved more people than just calamity-prone Lois Lane. The country was digging itself out of a depression and facing another world war. Unemployment was high, morale was low, and stress was everywhere. The timing was perfect for an author-artist duo from Ohio to introduce a caped do-gooder who championed the underdog. For ten cents, readers could escape to Metropolis, duck into a phone booth, and lose themselves in a fantasyland where the little guy always came out on top. The trip was short, but it helped millions of readers to cope with the tough times at home.

Superman turned fifty in 1988. Although the depression and the war are history, the Man of Steel was treated to a birthday ticker tape parade in Cleveland, a prime-time salute on television, and a place of honor in Macy's Thanksgiving gala in New York. Readers, it seemed, were still looking for an escape from anxieties—1990s style—and that meant Superman couldn't hang up his cape yet. He might have matured a lot in fifty years (back in '38, he couldn't fly and didn't have x-ray vision), but his mission was unchanged.

Even if you're not a fan of comic book heroes, chances are you have a favorite way of "getting away from it all." Hobbies, travel, films, and sports all provide short-term breaks in stressful routines. They're resources available for use as coping strategies. When pressures build, they serve as healthy escape hatches.

Our brains also have unique ways of dealing with anxiety, but they're not as harmless as getting lost in a good book or becoming

77

engrossed in the action of a close ball game. Called psychological defense mechanisms, they automatically kick in when we're faced with frustration, anxiety, and conflict. They alter our vision, cause us to look at ourselves through rose-colored glasses, and sometimes even blind us. They're the clever ways we deceive ourselves, protect ourselves, and extract ourselves from uncomfortable situations. In the end, we only kid ourselves. These are negative escape hatches that offer us temporary treatments for persistent problems. We all resort to them, and sometimes we do it several times a day.

Defense mechanisms (there are more than forty of them) aren't inherited but are learned very young. If you've ever watched the antics of a three-year-old child, you know how uninhibited emotions can be. If the toddler feels love, he offers big hugs and juicy kisses. If he's angry, he lets you know in no uncertain terms. If he hurts, he sobs and sniffles until the hurt goes away. Emotions surface, play themselves out, and disappear. It's refreshing to see.

Adults are different. We play games, and we rig the rules so that we always win. If we feel guilt, we somehow manage to transfer our guilt to someone else and make it *his* fault. We rationalize our behavior and justify our actions. In this way we can live with ourselves.

Why do we have such a great problem with defense mechanisms? The answer is found quite simply in understanding an important statement made by the prophet Jeremiah about the human heart:

> The heart is deceitful above all things,
> And desperately wicked;
> Who can know it?[1]

After dealing with literally thousands of counseling cases, we've come to the conclusion that understanding man's ability to deceive himself is the key to the appropriate approach to psychiatry.

As we think of the deceitfulness of man's heart, it's important to understand how people in the Old Testament viewed the heart. When Jeremiah, David, Moses, Samuel, or Solomon referred to the heart, they were not talking about the physical blood pump we refer to today. Just as we may use figures of speech such as "lose his head" or "blow his top," they too were using the heart in a figurative sense to speak of the immaterial person. In fact, an examination of all the references to the heart in the Old Testament—and there are scores—indicates that the heart was viewed as the seat of the human ability to think and reason, to feel, and even to make decisions. In short, it was the essence of human personality, intellect, emotions, and will. This is why Solomon's warning to guard your heart "with all diligence"[2] is so strategic. This explains Jeremiah's observation that God searches and tests the heart, an observation verified by David and Solomon.[3] It is important for us to gain insight into the hidden emotions and motives of the heart.

Perhaps David underscored the concept most vividly. For example, in considering God's revelation from nature, "the heavens declare the glory of God," and in Scripture, David concludes with the thought:

> Let the words of my mouth and the meditation of my heart
> Be acceptable in your sight,
> O, Lord.[4]

After contemplating God's presence in his life and in the universe, and the amazing and intricate detail in which he was created, even commenting on the intricate and complex design of his person "while in his mother's womb," he concludes:

> Search me, O, God, and know my heart;
> Try me, and know my anxieties;
> And see if there is any wicked way in me,
> And lead me in the way everlasting.[5]

Another extremely significant observation by David comes during his prayer for God's forgiveness following his fall into sin with Bathsheba. In Psalm 51:6, David prays, "Behold, You desire truth in the inward parts, / And in the hidden part You will make me to know wisdom." In essence, David's statement reflects our desperate necessity to be honest in our inward emotions and motives. In this case, he means the emotions that led him down the road to the immoral relationship with another man's wife. Moments later, David asks God to create within him a "clean heart and a right spirit."

Solomon, with all his wisdom, points out in Proverbs 23:7 that as man "thinks in his heart, so is he." On two occasions Jesus observed that "out of the abundance of the heart the mouth speaks."[6] In fact, in response to the religious leaders of his day, who were primarily concerned with what people did and ate and what religious ceremonies they carried out, Jesus said that it is not so much what you eat that defiles you, or what you take in, but rather what comes out of your mouth in evidence of the evil thoughts in your heart.[7]

How do we gain insight into these evil or inappropriate emotions and motives? One primary tool provided for us is Scripture. Hebrews 4:12 points out that Scripture is like a surgeon's scalpel, exposing the thoughts and motives of the heart. We live in a relative world; we tend to give ourselves the benefit of the doubt when we shouldn't. God's Word can tell us if our thoughts or motives are right or wrong.

Another helpful way to discern our thoughts and motives is through the encouragement or exhortation of friends. Hebrews 3:13 says, "Exhort one another daily, while it is called 'Today,' lest any of you be hardened through the deceitfulness of sin."

Selfish and sinful emotions and motives can creep into our lives and leave us calloused. This is wrong. That callous or hard edge on our hearts contributes to overall anxiety. God is pushing from within to make us aware of those wrong emotions and motives, and we're using the hard edge to suppress or hold down those thoughts. The tension created in this situation is anxiety. Many times the encouragement, direction, or insight given us by a good friend can make us aware of areas of blindness or nearsightedness and of the defense mechanisms that we may be using to keep us from looking at the painful reality of the truth.

One difference that sets Christian counseling apart from other counseling approaches is that Christian counselors believe defense mechanisms can be unhealthy coverups that may do more harm than good. They are involuntary ways people deceive themselves to ease their pain. You might say they're nature's built-in buffers, used to protect people from the truth they don't want to face. The philosophy goes like this: If the mind subconsciously covers up the truth, the truth doesn't go away, but at least it's out of sight. As the saying goes, out of sight, out of mind . . . or, out of mind, out of sight. Many secular counselors applaud this point of view because they believe defense mechanisms can prevent insanity since they are escape hatches from truth painful enough to cause permanent damage.

We don't agree. We believe it's healthier to endure the pain of truth long enough to heal the wound that is causing the pain.* While many people deceive themselves in an effort to ease anxiety (remember, anxiety comes from a fear of looking at the truth), the strategy often backfires. When people deceive themselves they actually may *cause* anxiety instead. Consciously they're protected from the truth, but subconsciously they know the truth anyway. The internal conflict that results causes fireworks, otherwise known as extreme anxiety.

Hide and Seek

To overcome anxiety successfully, each of us needs to know what defense mechanisms are, the forms they take, and the tricky ways they work. Armed with that knowledge, anyone can go on his own search-and-destroy missions. He can recognize the coverups when they appear, expose them for what they are, and look at the truth they're trying to hide.

Certain personality types seem to like certain defense mechanisms and rely on them frequently. For instance, people who have histrionic personalities (impulsive, dramatic, outgoing) often use a

---

*However, it is important to recognize that insight, learning the truth, needs to occur over a period of time rather than instantaneously.

defense mechanism called *somatization,* which allows them to cover up negative feelings such as anger with physical symptoms such as headaches.

As an example of somatization, let's look at Tony B., a former patient of ours who was a public relations executive for a Fortune 500 company. Tony was very creative, although if you asked his very conservative boss, you might hear that Tony was a bit *too* flamboyant. He was always coming up with colorful campaigns to promote the company image. His boss invariably pared down Tony's plan, eliminated the excitement, and deflated Tony's ego all in one brush. However, Tony never confronted his boss because he didn't want to jeopardize his career. Instead, he bit his tongue and suppressed his anger. His body reacted with a tightness in the muscles of his lower back. His blood vessels constricted, and he experienced severe headaches. Before long his health, not his anger, was the issue. His physical problems became so persistent that he never had the time or energy to think about any negative feelings toward his boss. If anyone had asked Tony point blank, "Are you angry?" he would have denied it vehemently.

"Why should I be angry?" he asked us, bewildered, during an early counseling session. Of course, even as he shook his head, he simultaneously twisted uncomfortably in the overstuffed chair we had provided him, and he searched his coat jacket for his bottle of aspirin. "Back trouble," he explained as he took several of the pills.

Tony's mind had deceived him into thinking that his problems were physical not emotional. His mind convinced him that he wasn't angry; he had a bad back. His headaches made him miserable, not his boss. Up to a point, the defense mechanism—somatization—was successful. It prevented his anger from surfacing, it headed off any confrontations with his boss, it secured his job, and on the surface it preserved his happy-go-lucky demeanor. But eventually the mechanism became an anxiety producer in its own right. The backaches and headaches that at first diverted his attention away from his anger now caused him real pain and new worry. The deception had certainly worked, but it wasn't a permanent fix.

We've all heard the promise that the truth will set us free. The trouble is that the truth can also hurt when we finally get around to facing it. Sometimes the truth not only causes us to acknowledge something we'd rather ignore, but it forces us to make decisions we'd rather postpone. In Tony's case, he had two bits of unpleasant business to attend to: He had to admit to the intense anger he felt; then he had to decide what he was going to do about it. Was he going to have a showdown with his boss, explain that he felt creatively stifled, and demand that the situation be changed? Was he going to realize that his talents would be put to better use by another company and therefore quit his job? Or was he going to concede that a conservative approach was appropriate for his employer and try to tune in to this position with enthusiasm and become a part of the team?

The choice was up to him. We merely pointed out that any solution to the problem was better than a flat denial that the problem existed.

Defense mechanisms such as the one used by Tony make people come across differently from what they are underneath. Tony was smiling on the outside and seething on the inside. What you saw was *not* what you got. The same is true of the rest of us.

In order to understand defense mechanisms fully, let's take a look at several of the most common ones. Some may seem familiar because you may use them to hide the truth you don't want to confront. Because there are so many, we'll merely highlight five and list the remaining ones in the appendix at the back of the book. Let's start with another favorite of histrionic personalities.

Denial

In that great Broadway musical *South Pacific,* heroine Nellie Forbush sings a show-stopping song called "Cock-eyed Optimist," in which she happily admits that she's "stuck like a dope with a thing called hope." Nellie's outlook is refreshing and positive because, while it's downright optimistic, it's also realistic. She's not blindly ignoring the real world, but is merely choosing to face the real world with an upbeat smile. That's determination, not denial. One is good; the other, bad.

Several years ago a study was done on a group of patients who were scheduled to undergo surgery. Although the procedure that the patients faced wasn't life-threatening, they were informed that any kind of surgery carries certain risks. As a matter of procedure, the doctors told the patients exactly what to expect, warned them what complications might occur, and described the worst scenario that could develop. Their purpose was to share all the possibilities so that there would be no surprises.

Each patient was rated on how he reacted to the presurgical briefing session. A follow-up interview was done after surgery to determine how each was handling the recovery process. As you might guess, some patients were gloom and doom, convinced that if something could go wrong, it surely would. Others totally refused to consider the possibility of a complication. They believed their team of doctors was infallible, and they waved off any talk of problems. Somewhere in the middle were the patients who expressed a genuine concern for the risks that were part of the surgery; they asked a lot of questions and wanted to be aware of as many clinical facts as they could comprehend.

Interestingly, the group that had the most difficult recovery period was the second—those patients who had refused to give thought or conversation to routine discomfort or unlikely complications. When confronted with the inescapable reality of postoperative pain, they expressed anger and disappointment. They couldn't deny the truth any longer because their bodies wouldn't let them. The group that handled recuperation the best was the group that had shown a legitimate concern about the surgery and the risks attached to it.[8]

Proverbs tells us that "The simple [person] believes every word, / But the prudent man considers well his steps."[9] Denial, as a defense mechanism, tricks a person into not looking at his thoughts, feelings, wishes, or motives. Some of the surgery patients refused to listen to the doctors' counseling. They would not consciously admit that, yes, they were concerned about what might happen and, yes, they had fears about what could go wrong. They blindly denied their feelings until the truth came crashing in around them. Then they had no choice but to accept the situation or to employ another defense mechanism such as rationalization.

Rationalization

Sour grapes. We've all used that expression at one time or other to cover hurt feelings and disappointment. When a young man, defeated in his bid for the senior class presidency, covers his crushed emotions by saying, "I really didn't want to win because being a class officer means you have to go to meetings all the time. I'd much rather be free to have fun my last year in school," he is demonstrating sour grapes. Rather than face the pain of rejection and the hurt of being denied something he wanted and worked for, he changes his point of view so he emerges a winner after all. He didn't *really* want to be class president, he convinces himself, and by losing the election he got what he wanted.

We can thank Aesop for the famous sour grapes line. Remember the fable about the fox who couldn't reach the grapes that he wanted so badly? Thwarted in his efforts to nab the fruit, he rationalized that it was probably sour anyway, and who wants to eat sour grapes?

Rationalization has been around a lot longer than Aesop's fables. As a defense mechanism, it's closely linked with denial. It's the mind's defense against embarrassment, disappointment, and many other anxiety-producing emotions. The mind changes its belief or viewpoint so that the person's feelings are no longer at odds with the situation. The surgical patients who suffered postoperative discomfort might have rationalized that they were being tested with pain to see how tough they were. They might have claimed to welcome the challenge in order to prove their mettle.

The Bible shows us many examples of godly men who rationalized negative behavior to make it seem positive. For example, Abraham thought that once the Egyptians saw Sarah, his beautiful wife, they would kill him and give Sarah to their pharaoh. He decided to lie to the Egyptians and tell them that Sarah was his sister, not his wife. He rationalized his willingness to hand over his wife to another man by convincing himself that it was for her sake. If he were alive he could still be close to Sarah and protect her. What good would he be to anyone if he were dead? This defense mechanism shielded him from feeling guilty. It allowed him to feel good about himself and to justify his bad behavior. It made his lie seem all right. [10]

Rationalization permits people to make adjustments in the way they look at events so that their behavior seems right in their eyes. But the Lord doesn't play such games. The wisest man who ever lived, King Solomon, realized this. He said, "Every man is right in his own eyes, / But the LORD weighs the hearts." [11] He looks past face-saving ploys and directly into the hearts to see the truth. We need to do the same.

Intellectualization

This common coverup is particularly popular among people who suffer severe inferiority complexes. A successful self-made man whose parents were not able to send him to college may continue to feel inferior to colleagues who boast an assortment of diplomas on their walls. To prop up his ego and make himself feel equal, he might speak in obscure, philosophical terms and employ long words to make his points. He might work hard to impress others as a means of impressing himself. To prove he has refined taste, he might surround himself with expensive works of art, and he might become a visible supporter of the local symphony and museum.

Although these activities seem very positive on the surface, they are motivated by a negative effort to hide the truth. People who use intellectualization as a defense mechanism often have difficulty making close friends because they are afraid friends will discover the truth about them. Also, potential friends may be put off by the smokescreen of lofty talk and boastful terms. If a counselor were consulted to help in the case of the self-made man, she would try to peel away the patient's intellectual facade. She would encourage him to look at his inferiority feelings and to recognize his sagging self-image. In the end, the patient would make peace with himself, accept himself, and thank God for the talents that enabled him to be a success. His support of the arts, one hopes, would continue, but now his motivation would be positive, not negative.

Intellectualization isn't all bad. In some professional settings it can have beneficial applications. For instance, a funeral director can detach himself from grief and prepare the body of an acquaintance for burial. He does this by concentrating on the intellectual aspect of mortuary science. His professionalism kicks in and prevents emotionalism from getting the better of him.

Identification

Another "either/or" defense mechanism—a response that can be either positive or negative—is identification. We've all heard about the importance of role models, and we've all read about the not-so-new phenomenon of mentoring. Up to a point identification can be positive; beyond that point it can become negative.

The apostle Paul urged the Philippians to "join in following my example, and note those who so walk, as you have us for a pattern."[12] It's interesting how over the years people have used the analogy of walking to describe the idea of one person's serving as an example for another person. We say a son "follows in his dad's footsteps" when the son chooses to attend the same school or enter the same profession as his father. We say a successor has "big shoes to fill" when he accepts a position previously held by someone who did a very good job.

Identification, as Paul depicts it, is positive. He wants us to identify people who lead godly lives, take note of how they walk their faith, and use them as examples as we make our own journey through life. The apostles modeled their "steps" after Jesus; people who became acquainted with the apostles modeled their lives after the apostles' ministries. In this way Christianity spread.

Identification becomes a negative defense mechanism when a person blindly patterns his behavior after someone who is not a positive role model. A child watches a violent drama on television and then begins to act aggressively. A teenager falls in with a bad crowd and feels the pressure to mimic the members' behavior. Insecure followers in a cult mindlessly tail after their leader, regardless of what direction he takes them.

To identify with another person and idealize that individual without thought or choice can be harmful. God meant for us to be aware of each other's actions, but He never meant for us to try to become a mirror image of anyone other than Christ. Instead, we've been given unique talents to explore and to expand as we glorify God.

Projection

This very common defense mechanism comes in two strengths—delusional and primary projection. The first, delusional, is more serious and can cause a patient to lose touch with reality. The second, primary projection, is less extreme and is used by nearly everyone. The mechanism gets its name because the person who uses it actually takes an emotion he is experiencing himself (anger, jealousy, lust, or guilt) and projects it onto another person; then he passes judgment on the other person for having the emotion. He self-righteously scolds someone else for his own shortcoming.

Perhaps the best example of delusional projection is the story of the stormy relationship between Saul and David in the Old Testament.[13] David burst on the scene and immediately won the admiration of Saul's servants, subjects, and son. Even Saul's daughter fell in love with the handsome young hero. Perhaps the last straw came when the women of Israel greeted their victorious king after battle with song and dance and chants that said, "Saul has slain his thousands, and David his ten thousands."[14]

Wait a minute, thought Saul as the numbers registered with him. *Thousands for the king and ten thousands for the upstart David?* From that moment on, Saul cast David in the role of villain and adversary. He falsely assumed that David was out to get him. He mistrusted and disliked David, so he assumed David mistrusted and disliked him. It wasn't true, but that didn't matter. He was convinced that David wanted to kill Saul (again, not true) when in actuality, Saul wanted (and persistently tried) to kill David. Had he been successful in murdering David, he could have *rationalized* that he was merely protecting himself.

Projection is another tricky way the mind eases a person's guilt. It allows the sinner to emerge as the good guy, while blame is shifted from one set of shoulders to another. As with all defense mechanisms, projection enables a person to fool himself part of the time. However, he can never—for *any* length of the time—fool the One who knows him best.

The human mind has a bag of tricks that succeed, at least for a little while, in covering up anxiety and preventing us from seeing clearly. These tricks are called defense mechanisms, and they're nothing more than deception. Deception is sin, and it doesn't take a Man of Steel with x-ray vision to recognize it. What it does take is a man of God to come to grips with it and determination and faith to overcome it.

Defense mechanisms sometimes are much easier to diagnose in other people than to recognize in ourselves. We can clearly see when someone else is denying the truth or shifting the blame or rationalizing some negative action. But our vision becomes clouded when we look within. We can say we're searching for the truth about ourselves, but we have difficulty being honest in our quest. Sometimes we need professional help to point out which defense mechanisms we're using and what truth these mechanisms are attempting to hide. In chapter 7 you'll meet a young woman who knew she was destroying herself by covering up painful emotions but was powerless to stop. She was beyond self-help methods and needed psychiatric care. She found it just in time.

Dealing with defense mechanisms is a two-step procedure. First, you must recognize that you are using a coverup. If you can't do that yourself, a counselor can guide you. Second, you must deal with the emotion that the mechanism is hiding. Again, a therapist may be needed if self-help techniques aren't successful. The important thing to remember is that coverups hide the truth, and truth is essential to healing. How you discover the truth—on your own or with professional counseling—is an important decision you have to make. Chapter 7 will help you make it.

7.

Self-Help or Professional Care?

IN THIS MOTIVATED, positive thinking, mind-over-matter society of ours, many people believe any obstacle can be overcome with sheer determination. And that includes anxiety.

The truth is, each of us can learn simple self-help techniques to ease tension, cope with worry, and prevent anxiety. In Part Three of this book we'll share several methods that we believe can lead to worry-free living. Included will be ten ways to prevent anxiety from recurring (chapter 9).

As beneficial as self-help techniques are, in some instances professional assistance and even hospitalization are needed if anxiety is to be successfully confronted and eventually conquered. When is medical care necessary? And what can be expected to occur behind the closed floors of a treatment center? Let's visit one of our medical units and meet a twenty-eight-year-old woman who probably would have died if she hadn't admitted herself into a facility and undergone intensive therapy for her severe anxiety disorder.

She is Cynthia Rowland, a television news reporter, who for twelve years led two lives. There was the public Cynthia, a bright, aggressive broadcast journalist on Channel 4, Little Rock; and there was the private Cynthia, a seriously ill bulimic who consumed up to twenty thousand calories and one hundred laxatives a day. On the surface she oozed self-confidence. In reality, she hated herself for the despicable habit she couldn't control.

When Cynthia came to our Richardson, Texas, treatment center in 1983, she was on a self-destruction course similar to that of a kamikaze pilot. Her life was in a tailspin, and her target, death, was dangerously close. If you had asked her what caused her problem, she would have blamed the "monster" that she said lived inside of her. She knew she had to conquer it before it killed her. She also knew she desperately needed help. She had battled the monster alone since she was seventeen, and she no longer could curb its demands. Her secret habit of binging and purging had once been weekly; now it was daily. Signs of anxiety were becoming more evident. Friends were beginning to notice her frequent periods of preoccupation, edginess, depression, and withdrawal. Her life was in danger because of her constant abuse to her body. Her electrolytes—important elements such as potassium and sodium that convey the body's electrical impulses—were severely out of balance.[1]

Cynthia suffered a double addiction—food and over-the-counter drugs. Her "habit" of overdosing wasn't illegal, so it was impossible to track or to treat without her consent. She often slipped out of the TV newsroom with a pocketful of coins and returned minutes later casually sipping a diet soft drink. Coworkers never suspected that her real purpose in visiting the bank of vending machines in the employees' break room was to consume a dozen candy bars. Neither did they guess that on the way back to her desk she would be overcome with guilt. She would duck into the restroom, wait until no one else was present, and force herself to vomit. They only saw her return to her typewriter, stopping en route to joke with the news director or to trade friendly barbs with the noontime anchorman.

Her status as a local celebrity sometimes got in the way of her destructive addiction. Often she would be recognized after work when she stopped at the supermarket to buy her evening's supply of snack foods, gallons of ice cream, and boxes of cookies. She quickly learned to rotate visits among several stores in order to avoid raising suspicions. She became masterful at lying. She would explain her purchase of two or three pizzas and dozens of dough-nuts by saying that an impromptu party was in progress or that she was buying dinner for the crew at work. Her svelte figure never hinted that all the food would be consumed by Cynthia herself. In public she restricted herself to salads and light dishes. She never seemed to be tempted by the junk food that other harried news reporters would gobble on the run.

Binge, Purge, Fast

Cynthia suffered from bulimia, one of several eating disorders that have attracted attention in the last decade because they seem to be symptomatic of a vain society preoccupied with appearances. America's fascination with the body beautiful is evident every time another diet book tops the best seller list or another video tape features a celebrity flexing her muscles to music.

The Journal of Family Practice conducted a survey a few years ago to determine the top concerns among teenagers, aged thirteen to eighteen. Sixty percent of the teens who were polled expressed a fear of being overweight. Only half of that number ever discussed their fear with a doctor. It's impossible to estimate how many of these young people resorted to the dangerous cycle of binging, purging, and fasting since problems such as bulimia often are "closet" diseases. Like many addictions, they are concealed by the victims who are caught in their snare.

While eating disorders are symptomatic, their causes are more serious than mere vanity. Cynthia's certainly was. Left unchecked, they can lead to a vitamin deficiency, chemical imbalance, organ dysfunction, or even death. Although four eating disorders have been identified by the medical profession, two are on the upswing: bulimia nervosa (an abnormal hunger for food) and anorexia nervosa (a lack of appetite for food).*

Bulimia nervosa and anorexia nervosa are anxiety related illnesses, as their names indicate; nervosa, the word they share, means "having to do with the nerves." Anorexia is more difficult to hide since it is characterized by extreme weight loss. Bulimia is definitely more common and, as in Cynthia Rowland's case, can be concealed for years.

Anorexia is overwhelmingly a woman's disease, with females

---

*Note: The other two disorders are known as pica, which is the repeated eating of a nonnutritive substance for at least one month; and rumination disorder of infancy, which is repeated regurgitation without nausea or associated gastrointestinal illness for at least one month.

accounting for 95 percent of its sufferers. Of these, about 2 percent eventually die from complications such as cardiac abnormalities. Because the anorexic's body has few calories to provide energy and sustenance, it feeds on the protein stored in the muscles. The heart muscle weakens and becomes vulnerable to infections.

When pop singer Karen Carpenter died in 1982 at age thirty-two, the cause of death was listed as heart failure. The sad truth was that she had been obsessed with her weight for more than twelve years. More fortunate was Cherry Boone O'Neill, daughter of Pat and Shirley Boone. Cherry suffered from both anorexia and bulimia for a decade before getting the help she needed to conquer the disease. Her weight dipped from 140 pounds to 80 pounds as she binged, purged, exercised for six hours a day, and took diet pills.[2]

Although their body weight is generally 15 percent below normal, anorexics often complain that they feel fat, and they become obsessed with worry that they will gain more weight. Consequently, they slowly starve themselves to death.

Bulimics appear to have the opposite problem. Rather than refusing nourishment, they repeatedly consume enormous amounts of food and then rid their bodies of the unwanted calories by either vomiting or using laxatives or diuretics. Often they subject their abused bodies to fasts while strenuously exercising to further trim their already slim figures.

A patient is clinically diagnosed as being bulimic when she binges twice a week for at least three months.[3] As many as 10 percent of college coeds may have bulimia, and this statistic is increasing. The upswing is not surprising since research done at Massachusetts General Hospital indicates about 80 percent of all adolescent girls have been on diets by the time they are eighteen.

For some women, being thin seems to be a lifetime preoccupation, but the price of maintaining an unrealistic weight can be high. Bulimics often develop a dependence on laxatives, have ulcers, and can even damage their teeth because of the acid contained in vomit.

Like anorexia, bulimia strikes mostly white females, particularly those who are between ages seventeen and thirty-six and are from financially comfortable families. The disorder should not be confused with everyone's normal tendency to overeat occasionally or with what the Bible refers to as the sin of gluttony. The true bulimic has a bona fide disease and frequently indulges in compulsive acts of uncontrollable eating and purging. This psychiatric problem is usually accompanied by depression, anxiety, and other psychological complaints.

Bulimia victims typically have obsessive personalities (see chapter 4), suffer low self-esteem, and work hard to earn the approval of everyone around them. They are literally dying to please and often are starved for attention and affection. They're perfectionists who cannot tolerate a less than-perfect physique. They believe that they are unattractive, and they work constantly to overcome their perceived shortcomings. As their condition worsens they become physically ill from the abuse their bodies sustain; they become mentally sick because of the guilt and shame they feel toward the horrible, secret habit they hide; and they become spiritually at odds because they think God is either punishing them or ignoring them because of their loathsome addiction.

Rx: Hospitalization Required

If someone has binged and purged even once, she (or he) should carefully study this book, as well as *The Monster Within* by Cynthia Rowland. If she binges and purges at all after that, then outpatient therapy should begin immediately before it becomes a compulsion. Outpatient therapy usually involves the individual's seeing a counselor for one 45-minute session a week, although some come more frequently to work on unresolved issues. The therapist serves as a mirror, giving the counselee insight into areas of blindness, defense mechanisms, or emotions of which she is unaware. Rather than just passively listening and grunting an occasional "uh-huh," or simply telling the counselee, "Here's what you do, and do it now," the counselor works with the counselee to formulate a plan for implementing the insights gained, new thought processes adopted, and new behavior patterns needed. Then in follow-up sessions, the counselor aids in progress review and fine-tuning, as well as in dealing with additional underlying roadblocks to mental and emotional stability which may be uncovered.

It is important to note, however, that when a bulimic, anorexia patient, or other severely impaired person reaches the point of being totally out of control, self-help techniques or outpatient counseling cannot solve the problem. If someone binges and purges once per week or more, hospitalization in a Christian eating disorder unit (like the Minirth-Meier Unit in the Dallas area) is urgent. The patient can be monitored around the clock while a carefully designed recovery program is implemented.

This was true of Cynthia, who required ten weeks of hospitalization before she was cured. She came to us just in time. She had reached her lowest point of depression on a Sunday, following a weekend binge that left her exhausted, swollen, and sick. She was tired of the cycle that kept repeating itself, and she was mapping plans for suicide when a friend who knew of her addiction called her on the telephone. The friend had attended church that morning and had heard a guest speaker explain her experiences as a bulimic and the treatment she had received at the Minirth-Meier Clinic. This friend convinced Cynthia to contact us. Although our unit was full, we determined from the conversation with Cynthia that an emergency existed, and she was immediately admitted to one of our Texas facilities.

Not all anxiety patients who are hospitalized are in life-or-death situations such as Cynthia's. Admission to a medical unit can be an option or a last resort. Some patients choose to enter a hospital simply because they know they can be helped faster by the concentrated care of an around-the-clock staff. Others prefer an outpatient program that enables them to continue to work and to meet family obligations while they see a counselor during prescribed times in an office setting. Another possibility is a type of combination of the first two. Called a "day hospital," it allows patients to spend mornings and afternoons in a clinic but to go home in the evenings. Each program has its advantages and drawbacks.

In at least three instances, hospitalization is not merely recommended, but is essential for the patient's well-being:

If the patient is out of control and could harm himself (frequent binging and purging can lead to sudden death from an electrolyte imbalance and/or other medical problems) or another person if allowed to continue functioning in society.

If medication must be frequently administered, monitored, and regulated by a professional medical staff.

If a treatment program must be implemented and overseen twenty-four hours a day. Most people can overcome bulimia in six to eight weeks of daily intensive hospital therapy, whereas outpatient therapy normally requires one to three years of weekly sessions and still may not be totally effective without the intensive insight-oriented approach and controlled, protective environment hospitalization affords.

Cynthia fit all three of the criteria for hospitalization. Her bouts with bulimia were frequent, and she could no longer stop the binge-purge cycle. The monster within her was clearly in control. Although she frequently promised herself she would overcome her addiction, she was powerless to do so. She continually pledged that tomorrow she would do better, but tomorrow never came. Her failure to make good on her promises to herself only increased her feelings of worthlessness and frustration.

She also needed immediate medical attention. After we put her through a complete battery of tests, including a CAT scan, EEG, and blood analysis, we discovered a serious vitamin deficiency. In addition to injections of vitamins, she needed a fiber supplement, a stool softener to help restore normal bowel activity, and antidepressants to correct her biochemical depression. Antidepressants are nonaddictive, and they ease the desire to binge and merely hide the serious symptoms of depression. Instead, antidepressants are nonaddicative, and they ease the desire to binge and purge. They also allow the patient to sleep restfully without awakening several times in the night with thoughts of suicide, worthlessness, and guilt. When the medication is no longer needed, the patient experiences no withdrawal symptoms.

Of course, particular attention had to be paid to Cynthia's diet. Not only did our staff have to plan menus that would be nutritious and soothing to her abused body, but we had to make sure that she ate the food that was prepared for her. We did this by measuring her intake and making sure she didn't purge it from her system. This meant a nurse had to sit with her during mealtimes and for an hour after she finished. She couldn't be trusted to visit the bathroom alone.

Equally important to her recovery were the mental and spiritual aspects of our program. Returning her body to normalcy would be a short-term "fix" at best if she didn't find and face the long-buried source of her anxiety and come to terms with it. This can be a lengthy process and usually requires a hospital stay of about six weeks, plus outpatient follow-up counseling for up to two years. In addition, national and community support is available through such groups as the Associates for Bulimia and Related Disorders and the Bulimia Foundation of America.

Treatments for anxiety-related illnesses such as Cynthia's are not uniform. As we will see in later chapters, several approaches may be used by different staffs with different philosophies at different hospitals. Cynthia had consulted more than fifteen medical and counseling professionals in nine years before coming to us. Some were horrified to hear her account of binging and purging. This shocked reaction only confirmed her disdain toward herself. Their advice was of no help. They told her simply to "stop it." When she visited one Christian counselor, he suggested that if she were to believe more strongly in God, everything would be all right. He only convinced her that she lacked faith. Another doctor listened to her story and then announced his prescription for recovery: She needed a husband. This made her angry.[4]

We like to describe our approach as comprehensive. Each patient who enters one of our treatment centers is assigned a team of several specialists to work on her case. In the safe, controlled environment of the hospital, these professionals help the patient to explore her pain and fears. A physician is responsible for the medical management and supervision of the clinical treatment. A staff psychologist works with the patient in daily two-hour group therapy sessions and provides psychological testing and evaluations. A therapist is designated for daily hour-long, one-on-one sessions for the duration of the hospital stay. Not only does this therapy involve the patient, but at certain points it will include the patient's family. Members of the team meet frequently to discuss progress and strategy. The psychiatrist acts as overseer or "quarterback" for the total healing effort.

Initially, the team's goal is to correct any emergency medical problem. No patient is able to concentrate on finding the source of her anxiety if she is physically exhausted, is suffering from blinding migraine headaches, or is so depressed that she is unable to communicate. This is why medication is one of a psychiatrist's most valuable tools. A significant percentage of depression is caused by repressed anger. When a person holds in her rage, the brain's supply of two key chemicals—serotonin and norepinephrine—is depleted, and symptoms of depression result. The patient is listless, can't sleep, refuses to eat, and experiences heart palpitations. While medication can correct the chemical imbalance and therefore get rid of the symptoms of depression, it can't remove the anger that has caused the imbalance in the first place. Only the resolution that usually follows intensive therapy can do that. If a patient is put on medication but does not enter therapy, she may appear to be cured, but the cure only lasts as long as she takes her medicine. A combination of medication and counseling is the answer.

Often, as in Cynthia's case, the patient has no idea what is causing her problem. Together, she and her team have to probe her past, looking for clues that will lead to the explanation. This search involves a great deal of dialogue and some written assignments as well. Cynthia kept a daily journal, which became the basis of her book, *The Monster Within*. She recorded the moments when she felt the need to binge and purge, and then with the help of her therapist she tried to figure out what sparked the urge. At the suggestion of an occupational therapist, she drew pictures and shaped clay into images that gave insight into her feelings. Obvious signs of anger and resentment kept surfacing although Cynthia couldn't explain why.

Pieces of the complex puzzle gradually began to fit together, and a sharp picture emerged. Cynthia had always been a model child. She was pretty, smart, popular, and extremely self-reliant. It was as if she sensed the pressure on her busy parents and decided not to add to it. Her father spent a great deal of time on the road trying to raise funds for a struggling Christian college; her mother managed their home and supervised the family. Cynthia's brother required a lot of attention, so Cynthia decided her role was to take care of herself and not make waves. "No problem" was her motto, even when she had problems. Outwardly she gave the impression that she didn't want attention. She didn't need hugs, help with her homework, or special encouragement. Her parents sensed her independence, quietly backed away, and concentrated on their business and her brother. Subconsciously, Cynthia misread this to mean they didn't care about her.

If there was a pivotal event in her life, it came at age four when she was accidentally burned by boiling water from a vaporizer. She was rushed to the hospital for emergency treatment. In those days, medical personnel didn't realize the mental trauma a child suffers when separated from her parents. Today, parents are encouraged to stay at their children's side night and day to give emotional support. Cynthia's mother and father weren't allowed to be with her; instead, they paced up and down the corridor outside her door. Cynthia interpreted their absence as further proof of their rejection of her.

No one took time to explain to the frightened little girl where her parents were or why they couldn't be present when white-draped doctors stripped dead flesh from her inner thighs.[5] She didn't understand that this stripping was a necessary part of her treatment. Because the doctors touched parts of her body she knew were very personal, she felt she had somehow participated in something naughty. She never told her parents about it. Feelings of guilt, insecurity, rejection, and isolation resulted. Subconsciously, she was convinced that she was unwanted, unloved, and unattractive. She felt damaged. From that moment on, she worked tirelessly to make herself perfect so that everyone would accept her, love her, and think she was pretty. Of course, perfection included a beautifully trim body.

Unlocking the misunderstandings of the past led to Cynthia's final victory over her monster. Long talks, conducted under the guidance of the therapist, helped the Rowlands recognize their daughter's needs and helped Cynthia comprehend her parents' actions. The truth set them free. When Cynthia left the hospital, she didn't return to her television job but chose to help others battle bulimia. She founded the Bulimia Foundation of America and now speaks at seminars across the country.

Cynthia's story contains many lessons for persons who struggle with any kind of chronic anxiety. Victims don't have to be bulimic or anorexic to benefit from her experience.

First, no matter how serious a problem is and no matter how long it has been present, it usually can be overcome. Behavior can be changed, old habits can be broken, and healthier ones can be established. Unfortunately, the physical illnesses that may have sprung from the anxiety often cannot be cured. Serious damage may already have been done. If anxiety has given rise to a weakened heart, bleeding ulcers, or high blood pressure, the patient may be impaired for the rest of his life. This danger underscores the importance of getting help as soon as possible.

Second, Cynthia's case illustrates the fact that some anxiety-related diseases can only be cured with professional help. Fortunately for Cynthia, she realized she was out of control, and she was able to get medical attention. If a person is past the point of recognizing his problem and refuses to take the initiative to see a doctor, a friend or family member may have to act in his best interest. More about this will be discussed in chapter 11 ("Friends in Need").

Third, it's important to realize that severe anxiety disorders can occur among good Christians in loving families. Cynthia was a believer, and so were her parents. There was no cruelty or mistreatment involved. However, there was a lot of misunderstanding and a serious lack of communication. Several unresolved childhood conflicts had been stacked on top of each other until the burden became so heavy that Cynthia lost control. As each of these conflicts was brought to the surface and dealt with during therapy, it disappeared. Her burden became lighter. Her monster was tamed.

When Cynthia left us after ten weeks of hospitalization, she was physically, mentally, and spiritually healthier than she had been for most of her life. She had learned not just to be tolerant of herself and her imperfections, but to love herself. In one of our final sessions with her, we made her aware of the challenges she would face as she resumed life on the "outside." The world that she was re-entering hadn't changed. It was still full of temptations, disappointments, and pressures. However, *she* was different, and her perception of the world was different. She had to hold onto what she had learned in therapy and reinforce it with outpatient counseling. Some backsliding was predictable, even inevitable. She needed to know that God wouldn't give up on her if she fell down briefly; neither should she give up on herself.

"For we all stumble in many things," James wrote to first-century Christians.[6] The same observation is applicable today. We still stumble and make mistakes. The key is to learn from past errors and to grow. God doesn't expect perfection of anyone in this life, but he does expect progress. The word most commonly used for *perfect* in biblical times carried the meaning of "to mature." Recognizing a problem and seeking help are two important steps toward maturity.

Cynthia did. So can you.

Are You a Compulsive Eater?

Overeating not only is a *symptom* of anxiety, but it can become a *source* of anxiety if it leads to feelings of guilt, anger, and loss of self-esteem. The physical well-being of a person is at risk when overeating is complicated by the urge to purge (bulimia). The following true-false quiz will help determine if you are a compulsive eater.

1. I eat sensibly, sometimes sparingly, when I am with   T   F
others, but I binge when I'm alone.

2. I find myself spending a great deal of time thinking   T   F
about food.

3. I often eat when I'm not really hungry.   T   F

4. I look forward to the times when I can eat alone with no   T   F
   one looking at me or commenting on my intake.

5. I plan secret binges ahead of time.   T   F

6. I go on these binges for no obvious reason.   T   F

7. I feel guilty after I overeat.   T   F

8. My preoccupation with food is making me or the people   T   F
   around me unhappy.

9. I resent it when friends urge me to use my willpower to   T   F
   stop overeating.

10. I've tried dieting, but I fall short of my goals.   T   F

11. I've been treated professionally for overweight.   T   F

12. In spite of my past efforts, I believe I could diet success-   T   F
    fully if I chose to.

13. I eat to escape from problems.   T   F

14. My weight affects the way I live my life.   T   F

15. I crave food at certain times other than the usual meal   T   F
    times.

If you answered "True" to three or more of the questions, you may be a candidate for a compulsive eating disorder. See your physician. Other help is available through such reputable groups as Overeaters Anonymous, 2190 190th St., Torrance, CA 90504.

(Note: The above quiz is based on materials from Overeaters Anonymous.)

PART THREE

How to Prevent Anxiety from Recurring

8.

Eight Ways to Prevent Anxiety

EDITH BUNKER ONCE sputtered to her on-camera daughter, Gloria, and son-in-law, Mike, that "Archie just doesn't know how to worry without getting upset."

Not only was Archie unable to keep his anxiety to himself; he couldn't keep it all in the family. Millions of American television viewers shared in the suffering whenever Archie railed at Edith or ranted at Mike.

There's a bit of Bunker in all of us. Our anxiety shows in spite of our efforts to keep it under wraps. Like it or not, people around us are affected. Experts in body language tell us that even when we protest that we're coolly in control, our gestures can muddy our message. Our reactions speak louder than words. Listeners remember the tension in our voices long after they forget what we were trying to say. We can claim to be calm, but if we stutter when we speak or stumble as we pace, no one believes us.

At some time or other, we've all felt like Mark Twain when he was so distressed before his first public lecture in 1891 that he couldn't eat or sleep. As he repeatedly practiced his humorous speech, the jokes seemed to go more and more flat. The day of the talk approached, and he admitted to being the most "frightened creature on the Pacific Coast." By the time he faced his audience, his distress had grown to panic-attack proportions.

"I was bewildered by the fierce glare of lights, and quaking in every limb with a terror that seemed like to take my life away," said Twain.

Whether or not they realized it, both Archie and Mark Twain endured their stressful moments by practicing simple techniques that most psychiatrists and counselors recommend for overcoming anxiety. Archie talked through his problems and spouted his feelings. Twain reduced his fear of failure by preparing his lecture several days in advance and practicing it over and over again. Success resulted. Archie always resolved his dilemma by the time the show's credits rolled, and Twain went on to become a world-famous lecturer.

Dozens of reliable self-help techniques for overcoming anxiety exist. Some are quick fixes that can soothe within seconds. Others may require a long-term commitment or even a drastic change in lifestyle. Some address the physical health of an anxiety sufferer, while others deal with his mental and spiritual well-being. All techniques work together, and when integrated into a comprehensive coping strategy, they can drastically reduce anxiety levels. Let's look at ten proven methods that we believe can prevent anxiety from recurring. We'll concentrate on mental and spiritual self-help techniques since tips on achieving physical well-being will be shared in chapter 10.

Meditate Daily

How happy and mentally healthy is the average seminary student? That was the question we attempted to answer a few years ago when we recruited a group of seminarians to take part in a research project. We felt certain we knew the results even before we began. *Of course* persons studying for the ministry would be spiritually mature, emotionally well adjusted, blissfully happy, and in peak mental health, right? What's more, we were convinced that the longer a person had been a dedicated Christian, the better his or her mental health would be. To prove these assumptions we pulled together a battery of tests that probed the students' personalities and spiritual lives.

As the data started to pour in, we realized we were in for a surprise. First of all, there was little connection between the students' mental health and the number of years they had been Christians. Long-term commitment didn't guarantee inner peace. What proved to be more important was the number of years that the students had regularly meditated on Scripture. That made a big difference. If meditation had been a part of their lives for *at least three years*, they were significantly happier and healthier.

As Christians, we were pleased when this piece of information surfaced in our study. It told us that Scripture meditation works. We had proven that. But our findings didn't end with that conclusion. We found there are right and wrong ways to meditate on Scripture. Regularity may be a key factor, but spontaneity is another. Surprisingly, these factors are not at odds with each other.

In today's goal-oriented society too many of us are driven by good intentions and rigid objectives. We view Scripture meditation as just another item on our things-to-do list. Meditation can become a burden if we set daily levies on ourselves much as we do with pushups and jogging laps. Yet we all know people who boast that they read the Bible from cover to cover annually. It's even been mathematically determined that if you read the Bible at "pulpit rate," it requires less than twelve minutes a day to work your way through the entire text in a year. This bit of trivia often is followed by the challenge, "Can't *you* spare twelve minutes a day to spend with the Word?"

But reading isn't the same as meditating. Scripture meditation shouldn't be an obligation tied to a time line and routinely fulfilled without thought or preparation.

To boost the effectiveness of meditation, you need to follow certain guidelines. The environment should be quiet; you should be in a relaxed mood and should be sitting (or kneeling) in a comfortable place. No specific goal should be set as to the amount of reading you must complete in a given number of minutes. Instead, plan to spend about one-half hour reading, stopping, and meditating on any passage that seems to be meaningful at the moment. Tailor your reading by choosing verses that address your current concerns. For instance, if you're feeling particularly anxious, read one of the verses of reassurance in the New Testament: "My peace I give to you; not as the world gives do I give to you. Let not your heart be troubled, neither let it be afraid."[1]

Or if you feel guilty about something you've done, meditate on the verse: "As far as the east is from the west, so far has He removed our transgressions from us."[2] By controlling the situation you'll achieve maximum results from your meditation.

Many Bible verses underscore the importance of God's Word. For example, in the longest chapter in the Bible, in Psalm 119, almost every verse in some way emphasizes the priority of God's Word. Two clear examples in Psalm 119 point out how God's Word brings about cleansing (v. 9) and can prevent us from sinning (v. 11). Verse 89 is consistent with Jesus' statement in Matthew 24:35 regarding the permanent and eternal nature of God's Word. Verses 24 and 92 are consistent with Jeremiah's statement in Jeremiah 15:16 that a steady diet of God's Word can produce joy in the heart. Verse 32 parallels Joshua 1:8, indicating that success and the way of life are by-products of a regular intake of and obedience to the word of God. Verse 28 is consistent with 1 John 2:14 in its suggestion that personal strength comes with God's Word.

In short, the longest chapter in the Bible is in keeping with the Bible as a whole indicating the absolute priority of God's Word for mental, emotional, and spiritual strength and stability.

Condition Yourself to Relax

Often when we counsel anxious patients, we teach them to use a repetitive phrase to help them unwind. We suggest they say the same words over and over whenever they catch themselves worrying. This technique can work for you too.

At the first hint of anxiety, before the symptoms multiply and conquer you, try breathing deeply and slowly. Each time you exhale, repeat the same phrase. What words work best? It doesn't matter. Christians often like to use a favorite line of Scripture. Perhaps one of the verses that you've meditated on will hold a special meaning for you. If so, jot it down on an index card and carry it with you to memorize for use during stressful times. Or you can choose a phrase as simple as, "Anxiety is a signal to relax." It's a true statement; it has a certain balance and rhythm. And if you say it over and over whenever you are trying to reduce stress, you'll begin to link the words to the response that you want. Eventually the phrase will trigger the desired reaction automatically.

Some of the most successful uses of repetition can be found in any hymnal. A favorite song of ours is "Tell It to Jesus." Not only does the third verse reach out directly to persons who suffer anxiety—"Do you fear the gathering clouds of sorrow? . . . Are you anxious what shall be tomorrow?"—but the hymn's refrain is repeated twelve times: *"Tell it to Jesus, / Tell it to Jesus."*[3] The familiarity, the rhythm, and the repetition of the words have a healing and rejuvenating effect.

Time and conditioning are required before this method is dependable. When we teach patients to use the technique, we often repeat the chosen phrase fifty times during the first counseling session. As they begin to make the association between the words and the response, we can visibly see the results. Muscles relax, frowns soften, and voices become less tense. During subsequent sessions the phrase is repeated less often to get the same response. Finally, at the first mention of the phrase the patient noticeably relaxes. The association has become automatic.

Try it. Take the simple words "calm down" and repeat them slowly as you deeply breathe in and out. Inhale on "calm"; exhale on "down." As you say the phrase, turn your mind to the hillside that David talked about in Psalm 23, and concentrate on the calmness of the green pastures and the stillness of the waters. Close your eyes and escape to the peaceful setting.

Or try to visualize a favorite retreat. Spread your towel on a remote beach on the seashore or sit on a rocky perch in the mountains of Colorado. You get the idea. Return to a setting that led you to relax and vacation there a moment.

Listen to Soothing Music

Did you ever wonder why so many stores provide easy listening music during business hours? Why not rock? Why not heavy metal? Why not silence? The answer is that soft background music makes sense—and dollars. Sales increase when shoppers slow down, relax, browse, and enjoy themselves.

Music can generate stress or alleviate tension. If the sound is loud and the beat is throbbing, anxiety can be heightened. If the melody and rhythm are balanced, they can soothe the listener and calm anxiety.

Christian, classical, and contemporary ballads can also work effectively. No one knows this better than musicians themselves. When composer Robert Schumann was suffering from acute mental illness—first melancholy, then a severe sleep disorder, and finally hearing demon voices—his friend, Johannes Brahms, visited him in the asylum to quiet him with soft ballades. Another famous composer, Frédéric Chopin, accepted the fact that he was dying at age thirty-nine, but was tormented by the fear that he would be buried alive. One of his few pleasures was to listen to music. Shortly before his death, a well known opera singer visited him and sang his favorite Bellini aria. His anxiety subsided, at least for the moment.

The soothing effect of instrumental music has been known since biblical days. In the Old Testament, King Saul periodically suffered from what his servants called "a distressing spirit." They once asked his permission to find a skillful musician who could play a harp whenever Saul felt anxious. David was recruited for the assignment, and he was so successful that he became a permanent member of Saul's household. Whenever David was called to play his melodious music, the effect was immediate: "Then Saul would become refreshed and well, and the distressing spirit would depart from him."[4]

Talk Through Your Problems

Anxiety and depression build because people don't air their feelings daily. Linda J. in chapter 1 is an excellent example of what can happen to someone who tries to deny anger and frustration over a long period of time. We psychiatrists tell our patients to ventilate their anxiety. A small problem can become a phobia if it's turned inward and allowed to fester. So let it out. Communicate.

Of course, rules exist. (See "Guidelines for 'Fighting Fair,'" p. 167.) The Old Testament tells us that it's all right to confront our neighbor if we're angry, but that doesn't give us the right to lash out at him cruelly, hold a grudge against him, or direct some kind of get-even tactic toward him. Any confrontation should be done quickly so that forgiveness can begin. Also, while the conflict may never be completely forgotten, it should be disposed of permanently and not revived and tacked onto every new problem that surfaces.

Just as we agree to speak our minds, we should also pledge to listen to the other person's feelings. Unfortunately, listening is one communication skill that is seldom taught and often overlooked. We're thoroughly schooled in how to deliver information but not how to receive it effectively.

A study was once done to determine the amount of time that managers and other professional people spend in communication. Here's what was learned: While busy people devote 80 percent of their day to communicating, most of those hours are spent listening. The breakdown was 45 percent listening, 30 percent talking, 16 percent writing, and 9 percent reading.

Too often we reward the talkers and champion the person who "got in the last word." Effective ventilation of feelings is based on open circulation. Anxiety diminishes when words flow freely in all directions.

Limit Your Worry

As counselors, we come in contact with a lot of professional worriers. Their productivity suffers because so much of their time is wasted and their energy sapped by constant fretting. If only they could schedule their worry for a specific time slot, confine it to that period, and not allow it to distract them from other matters! Is it possible? Yes, and while the method may sound silly, it works well, particularly for people who are perfectionists.

We suggest setting aside fifteen minutes in the morning and another fifteen minutes in the evening for active worry. If concerns surface during other times of the day, the person should jot them down on a card and vow to deal with them during the designated period. Worry-free living involves confining the natural worry we all feel into a designated time slot of only 1 percent of a twelve-hour day.

Three positive results come from this exercise. First, the person accomplishes a great deal more during the day when he is free of anxiety's tug. Second, when "worry time" finally arrives, he's better able to deal with his problems because he feels good about his productive day. He now can devote his total attention to his worries, and he can list them according to seriousness. Third, and a key benefit, will be that by the time he looks at the problems they often will have shrunk in importance, and the cards and the problems can be tossed aside.

Live One Day at a Time

Persons who are anxious spend much of their time worrying about the future and playing "what if" games. On the other hand, people who suffer depression are stalled in the past and waste much of their present playing "if only" games. For these reasons, the suggestion to take one day at a time may seem impossible to follow.

An average person gets up in the morning and may have three items to accomplish in the course of the day. He may complete two of the three, doing one right and the second wrong. Still, he shrugs it off as "no big deal." The perfectionist gets up in the morning with a list of twenty tasks to complete. If he achieves nineteen of the twenty, he is dissatisfied with himself. He's guilt ridden because he feels he's fallen short. He doesn't stop to realize that his goals were unrealistic and had him programmed for failure. If he had managed to accomplish all twenty items, he probably would have felt his objectives weren't challenging enough. The next day's list might have included twenty-one tasks. In both cases, anxiety is the result, either from his failure to set tough goals or his failure to meet the goals he set.

In the hit Broadway play and the film *Annie,* the little red-haired, orphaned heroine looks forward to tomorrow with the words, "You're only a day away." The idea is that everything will be better, brighter, more secure, and less harried in the future. But constant anticipation breeds constant anxiety. The future never measures up to its expectations.

What about today? Jesus advises us, "Therefore do not worry about tomorrow, for tomorrow will worry about its own things. Sufficient for the day is its own trouble."[5]

Design an Action Plan

When Mark Twain faced the task of delivering that humorous speech to the standing-room-only audience, he was nearly overcome with anxiety. What could he do about it? He had three options: He could cancel the obligation and disappoint everyone; he could continue to wring his hands in misery and let anxiety compound anxiety; or he could write a speech and practice it repeatedly. He chose action plan #3.

The point is this: Do *something* to lessen your anxiety. Don't just agonize over your circumstances. If you're worried about failing a test in school, work out a study plan to prepare yourself for any question your teacher might ask. If you're anxious about entertaining your husband's boss for dinner, ease the pressure by choosing a fix-ahead menu, arrange to have your children stay overnight with your best friend, order a pretty floral centerpiece, and prepare the table hours in advance. Study the options, select a plan, and then implement it.

We once counseled a very successful Christian businessman in ways he could shake his anxiety so that he could deliver his strong testimony to a large group. He told us early in our sessions that when he was a young boy he and his father had had a strained relationship. His father had expected him always to excel, and the son felt he never quite satisfied those expectations. This lack of confidence spilled into his adult life and caused him tremendous stress whenever he faced an audience.

We helped him look at his options. We pointed out that he either could refuse invitations to speak and pass up opportunities to lead people to Christ, or he could prepare his message so thoroughly that he'd have confidence in its content if not in himself.

"Concentrate on the positive benefits to others," we suggested. "Dig into the Bible for the heart of your message, and then pull illustrations from your life to give it a contemporary and personal touch. Get involved with your words. Forget about yourself and think about how you might help others. Practice in front of the mirror until you're comfortable with your mannerisms. Seek honest and positive feedback from a good friend. If anxiety starts to build before your introduction, ask yourself, 'What's the worst thing that could happen?' Maybe they won't ask you to come back. Maybe you won't be paid an honorarium. Maybe the applause will be polite but not thunderous. None of these consequences is life-threatening. You'll survive!" He did: The result was success.

Cultivate the Awareness of God's Presence with You

The best antidote to anxiety available to all of us is the knowledge that God is with us. The importance of an awareness of God's presence is underscored from the life of Moses in Hebrews 11:27: "He endured as seeing Him who is invisible." For Moses, the reality of God's presence was as tangible as if he could reach out and touch or view God at any moment.

A familiar story tells of a devoted Christian who died and went to heaven and finally sat face to face with Jesus.

"I've waited so long for this moment," said the man. "At last I'm in Your presence."

"But you've always been in My presence," answered the Lord. "Look at the earth below and see your footprints where you walked during your lifetime."

The man looked down and saw two sets of footprints side by side in the sand, over rocks, and through a clearing.

"I recognize my footprints," said the man. "But who was walking next to me?"

"I never left your side," said Jesus.

The man squinted and saw several areas of particularly rough terrain where only one pair of prints was visible.

"I don't understand," began the man. "In some places—the difficult places—I can only see a single set of tracks."

"Those are my footprints," explained the Lord. "Those were the times when I carried you."

In the Bible, the prophet Elisha once found himself in an extremely difficult predicament. The king of Syria wanted to capture him and had sent his army to surround the city in Israel where Elisha was living. When Elisha's servant went out in the morning and saw the mounted soldiers with their weapons and chariots, he was filled with anxiety. "What shall we do?" he asked Elisha.

The prophet calmed the servant by explaining that with God as their ally, they were invincible. They had more power working for them than their enemy could muster to work against them. To help the servant fully understand the awesome protection that God provides His people, Elisha prayed that the young man's eyes might be opened. God granted the prayer, and the servant looked outside to see the mountains filled with God's horses and ablaze with His chariots of fire.[6]

Anxiety can be an enemy just as real and as devastating as the armed soldiers that threatened Elisha. It can cripple and it can kill its victims. It can also be disarmed and conquered when we stop and remember that we are not alone. The Man whose footprints accompany ours has greater strength than ours or our opposition's. He can protect us and prop us up. He can even carry us.

Determine You Will Obey God

As psychiatrists, we know that a great deal of anxiety is caused by guilt. Tension builds when people experience an internal tug between right and wrong. Their Christian background has instilled in them a moral code. They know what they should do (the "right") and they know what they want to do (the "wrong"). Their flesh is pulling them one way; their conscience is tugging in an opposite direction. Anxiety grows as this private struggle continues. If the flesh wins over the conscience, guilt takes hold and anxiety increases.

God doesn't want us to suffer anxiety. In fact, He commands

us to "be anxious for nothing."[7] This is not a suggestion or a request. It is an order from God. In Matthew 6:25–34, Christ used the word *worry* six times, and half of those times He used it as part of an order. *Do not worry* about food, about clothes, about tomorrow, about your life, He told His disciples.

To overcome anxiety and eliminate guilt we need to obey God in two important ways. First, we need to call a halt to the internal tug of war that exists between our conscience and our flesh. Tension is eliminated when we make the right choice. Second, we need to make a conscious decision to follow God's explicit order not to worry. To continue to fret is a direct denial of a commandment from God.

Replace Worry with Prayer

Prayer is an important priority in fighting anxiety, particularly when coupled with time in the Word and insight and feedback from friends.[8] If your worry is linked to fear—you're afraid of some situation you're about to face—pray that God will help you through the ordeal. Be specific in your request. Pour out your dilemma and ask for His guidance.

If your worry is unknown—you feel tense but you don't know why—ask for insight. Pray that God will search you and show you what the source of your anxiety is so that you can address it quickly.

The most effective approach to overcoming anxiety is a multi-pronged plan that blends positive praying with positive thinking, followed by positive action. Positive praying simply means thanking God for His solution before your problem is solved. Positive thinking involves looking at the problem realistically with an eye for what can be learned and gained from it. Positive action is taking the first steps toward a solution.

As an example, let's look at Paula, a friend of ours who was laid off from her teaching position because of her school district's shrinking enrollment. She could have been depressed by the unexpected "pink slip" that accompanied one of her final paychecks. She might have been angry since her dismissal was based on lack of seniority and not on lack of ability. She could have resented her principal, fellow teachers, and the community. Instead, she chose a multipronged, positive approach.

Her first response was to pray to God, explain that she was anxious about her lack of income, and thank Him in advance for the job opportunities that would surely surface for her good and His glory. Her second act was to focus on the possibility of going to graduate school for additional training or relocating to a different part of the country where a teacher shortage existed or immersing herself in volunteer work until she found another teaching job. Finally, her action plan involved going to the library and studying several education journals and jotting down job openings. Next, she updated her resume and sent away for a catalog from a nearby university.

By choosing to deal with her situation in a positive manner, Paula suffered only slight anxiety. She still had her problem, but she was facing it with inner peace and calm demeanor. Her ability to face difficulty without the negative emotions of anger or bitterness impressed those people who received copies of her resume. In the end, she was faced with a new dilemma: which of three job offers she should accept.

More Help Is Available

Of course, many levels of help are available beyond the techniques we've shared in this chapter. For some people the answer is counseling and psychotherapy to get at the core issues behind anxiety. So often we are unaware of those emotions or motives which may be trying to force their way up from the subconscious into the conscious. God's spirit may be pushing them up to make us aware of what David termed "secret sins."

Many times the encouragement and counsel available from a good friend, a lay or pastoral counselor, a psychologist, a psychotherapist or psychiatrist, depending on the level of anxiety and need, can put us in touch with the core issues and help us develop a plan to deal with them in a way that will siphon off anxiety.

If a problem persists, another solution may involve coming to grips with faulty belief systems. For example, many people experience ongoing anxiety because they have bought into certain irrational and untrue beliefs about themselves and the world they live in. One such belief is perfectionism, which is the mistaken notion that we need to do everything flawlessly.

Another common irrational misconception is approval addiction, best explained as the feeling that we must be loved by almost everyone. Other common irrational beliefs are the ideas that it is a catastrophe when life doesn't unfold as we prefer it to do or that personal unhappiness is caused by external circumstances or that we cannot control negative feelings or that it's easier to avoid life's problems than to assume responsibility and take action.

These irrational beliefs often lead to distorted forms of thinking in a given situation. For example, we've all heard the expression "making a mountain out of a molehill" or, as we would call it, magnification. Perhaps someone makes a slightly negative comment about us and we remain angry the rest of the day. For a five-cent remark, we return a five-dollar anger. Another common cognitive distortion is the all or nothing, black or white polarization. For instance, if you're driving down the freeway and someone cuts you off, you conclude that the driver is completely worthless.[9]

Part of the comprehensive approach that we take at the Minirth-Meier Clinic is to provide our hospital patients with one hour per day of cognitive therapy seven days a week. A cognitive therapy specialist works on a process that is described in Romans 12:2 as "the renewing of your mind." They go over and over fallacies the patient clings to, and they seek to erase those negative tapes and replace them with more appropriate and accurate data. As Jesus said, "You shall know the truth, and the truth shall make you free."[10] Freedom from anxiety often is the direct result of gaining insight into these faulty belief systems.

Finally, we can't overlook the fact that in some cases patients need appropriate medication (see appendix 4). The decision as to whether or not medication should be prescribed and what type would be most beneficial can only be made in conjunction with a psychiatrist who is properly trained in the use of psychiatric medications.

Stayed Tuned . . .

The severity of the anxiety will determine if the first level of care (self-help) is sufficient or if the second level of care (professional assistance) is needed. In either case, emotional health is an attainable goal, and it can be achieved more quickly and effectively if the anxious person adopts and maintains a balanced lifestyle. What are the components of such a lifestyle? We'll examine them in the next chapter.

9.

The Balanced Lifestyle

THE MENTAL AND spiritual self-help techniques shared in chapter 9 are only half of the comprehensive coping strategy that we recommend to prevent anxiety. The other half is physical, and requires dedication, stamina, and—believe it or not—management skills.

Let's be honest. No matter how dedicated you may be to physical fitness and wellness, several factors related to your body and its ability to overcome anxiety are beyond your control. For instance, everyone's body ages, and so far, no one (except sci-fi writers) has figured out a way to reverse that process. Also, you can do nothing about your genetic makeup except be aware of it and be prepared for what may be an unfortunate family tradition. Like it or not, heredity may make you vulnerable to certain diseases. Another irreversible factor that carries predictabilities, both biological and social, is gender. Women will always bear the trauma of childbirth and risk the misery of post-partum blues, while social tradition makes men the more likely candidates for battle fatigue and workaholism.

The good news is that four factors are within your control and have a great deal of impact on how fit for the fight you are: sleep, diet, recreation, and exercise. Your *management* of these four fitness factors influences how successfully you respond to anxiety.

Managing to Stay Fit

Time management. Stress management. Change management. Conflict management. Career management. Human resources management. Surely one of the most popular buzzwords in recent years has been the term *management*. Tack it on to any noun and suddenly that noun becomes a science, complete with its own experts, textbooks, seminars, and motivational tapes.

A manager is anyone who has ongoing control of, authority over, and responsibility for a function or an organization. Using that definition, every man, woman, and child is a manager. Each of us has control of, authority over, and responsibility for our physical, mental, and spiritual health. Our "organization" is the finely tuned, meticulously designed, God-given power plant, the human body.

Here's how Dr. Fred Hooper described the awesome task each of us has of managing the body and maintaining its condition:

> Have you ever paused long enough to consider the responsibility that you have to yourself? You are responsible for . . .
> Several hundred million cells.
> 10 billion nerve cells.
> 60,000 miles of blood vessels.
> A heart that pumps 2,000 gallons per day.
> Kidneys that filter 2,500 pints of blood per day.
> Lungs that inhale/exhale 500 cubic feet of air per day.
> A skeletal system made up of more than 200 bones.
> A muscular system made up of more than 650 voluntary muscles and countless involuntary muscles that control everything from heart beat to 'goosebumps.'[1]

If this sounds like a full-time job, it is, and it lasts a lifetime, twenty-four hours a day; yet it offers no salary and includes no retirement plan. In fact, your length of service depends to a great extent on how good a manager you are. A healthy body that has been carefully supervised can withstand the external challenges of sickness and disease and the internal threats of stress and anxiety for more than seventy years. The benefits are enormous: Happiness is the long-term payback for a job well done.

In chapter 8 we outlined ten mental and spiritual techniques you could use to obtain worry-free living. In this chapter we will explain the second part of the self-help strategy. We will discuss how the careful management of your body's physical well-being can bolster your efforts to reduce stress and eliminate worry. Anxiety and physical fitness are closely related. When your mind and body are strong, you are less vulnerable to stress. Even if anxiety is inevitable—which it often is—its long-term effects will be fewer if you are fit to be tried. Physical fitness involves establishing healthy resting, eating, recreation, and exercise habits. Let's look at each, beginning with (sh-h-h-h) sleeping.

Forty Winks and Counting . . .

Sleep has been a mystery to humanity ever since Adam nodded off in the Garden of Eden and awoke to find he had lost a rib and gained a companion. From that day forward it has been both blessed and cursed. Workaholic Ben Franklin once grumbled to a friend, "Up, sluggard, and waste not life; in the grave will be sleeping enough." Shakespeare was more charitable, calling sleep "nature's soft nurse." Job complained about his lack of sleep: "I have had my fill of tossing till dawn"; and Aristotle philosophized that sleep is society's great equalizer since "All men are alike when asleep."

Even today sleep is clouded with questions and continues to draw mixed reviews from critics and fans. Psychiatrists agree that it can be a problem (some people complain they don't sleep enough while others say they sleep too much) or it can be a solution to a problem. "You'll feel better in the morning" is a favorite assurance many of us use when we can't think of anything more clever to say. Sleep raises questions: Is an inability to sleep the result of a disturbed body or a sign of a troubled mind? Or it can provide answers: Dream analysis is a tool used by many psychiatrists during insight therapy.

In spite of the ongoing mystery, we're learning more about sleep every day. We know, for instance, that sleep is not a sluggard's waste of time as Ben Franklin suggested and that the average person needs to sleep for a third of his life. Variations occur, of course, depending on age and lifestyle. Newborn babies sleep about eighteen to twenty hours a day and dream for half that time. Less sleep is required as children age, with twice-a-day naps slowly giving way to short afternoon snoozes and finally diminishing to no rest period at all. Usually sleep patterns stabilize during the late teen years when seven to eight hours per night is recommended. This decreases slightly later in life. Senior citizens often need less sleep and tend to sleep more lightly as they age, partly for physical reasons such as the discomforts of arthritis or rheumatism and the more frequent need to use the bathroom.

Although many people argue that they don't need much sleep and boast that they easily can get by on four or five hours a night, they may be putting themselves at risk. The body and mind desperately need the natural suspension of consciousness that occurs during sleep. Energy is renewed, brain chemicals are metabolized, and muscles are totally relaxed. The belief that rest without sleep is just as rejuvenating as sleep simply is not true. The person who gets less than four or five hours of sleep per night over an extended time actually has increased by seven his chance of dying at any time.[2]

Getting enough sleep makes an enormous difference in being able to cope with what is going on in your life. When you aren't rested, you can become irritable, experience personality changes, or even become psychotic (extreme mental illness). A person who is overly tired often cries very easily, doesn't want to eat, loses his mental and muscular quickness, is bothered by constipation, and is a likely target for infections.

Many of these symptoms surfaced during World War II in the Allied and the Axis military camps and on the homefront. The British tried to increase their efficiency by extending the work week so they could produce more war supplies. Up to a point, they were successful. But when the week was stretched beyond fifty-four hours, productivity decreased. The workforce was tired, and what began positively ended negatively. On the other side of the conflict, the enemy was withholding sleep to get our soldiers to share war secrets. American POWs were repeatedly awakened as soon as they fell asleep. They became disoriented and exhausted and experienced serious mental problems. The effect was as devastating as the one shown in the stock television drama that depicts an accused criminal being interrogated for hours under a blinding lightbulb.

No matter how strong the person is in the beginning, without sleep he eventually cracks.

This same link between sleep, anxiety, and mental illness is evident in the Old Testament account of an exhausted Elijah collapsing in the wilderness and praying to God to let him die. He was mentally and physically worn out by his grueling escape from Jezebel's murder threats. He was alone, his body ached, and he had no will to continue. In this frame of mind, he begged God to take his life. It's important to note that God's treatment didn't begin with talk or advice. First there was sleep, then food, then more sleep. Only after he was completely refreshed and had taken the physical steps to shake his depression did God allow Elijah to continue the forty-day trek to the mountain.[3]

History has taught us the value of sleep, and we're reminded of it every day in our medical practice. We often prescribe total rest as the first phase of treatment for patients hospitalized for anxiety disorders. The story unfolds this way: The person comes to us depressed, uptight, and sometimes suicidal. As we jot down his medical history, we learn that he hasn't had a good night's rest in weeks. He's in no condition to be counseled or to take part in any kind of therapy. He simply can't concentrate. So we put him to bed for a day or two. The results are amazing.

"You've done so much for me already," he'll say, usually surprised. "I can't believe how much better I feel."

Actually we've done nothing more than help his body get the rest it craves. Only then can we get down to the serious business of healing. As we identify the source of the anxiety and we work to expose and overcome it, the need for the sleeping pills diminishes. They've served their purpose by allowing the body to strengthen itself until it no longer hinders our attempts to treat the emotions.

Of course, you don't have to suffer severe anxiety to have bouts with insomnia, and you don't need medication to conquer it. More than half of all Americans complain of it at some point in their lives, and if you are one of them, take heart. You're in good company. The persons most prone to sleeplessness are good, hardworking, overly conscientious people—like you.

So what can you do about it?

First of all, try not to worry about it. We've all heard of the "vicious circle," and this is a classic case. Anxiety and stress cause insomnia, and insomnia causes more anxiety and stress. Don't panic and think that you have to *make* sleep happen. Instead, relax and *let* it happen. In fact, sometimes we actually urge our patients to try to stay awake. This is called paradoxical intention. We find that when persons make an effort to stay awake, they often fall asleep.

It's helpful to go to bed at about the same time every night. Anyone who has ever traveled to Europe or another far-off destination knows about jet lag. Sometimes our bodies need several days to adjust themselves to being awake when they're in the habit of being asleep. Everyone has a biological clock and a natural bodily rhythm. You need to tune into yours. Know if you're a "morning person" or a "night person," and make sure you adjust your schedule on both sides of the clock to get your required eight hours of sleep.

And speaking of clocks, your alarm clock shouldn't have to wake you every morning. If it is, you may not be getting enough sleep. A truly rested person usually awakens before the alarm goes off. Of course the amount of stress and anxiety you've endured in a day will determine if you need seven or eight or even nine hours of sleep. The need will vary.

Other bits of advice that will *let* sleep happen are:

- Don't exercise right before going to bed.
- Limit your intake of caffeine to less than 600 milligrams a day.
- Avoid taking a stack of work to bed with you; a novel or magazine, yes. But financial reports or sales figures? Never.
- Avoid eating a heavy meal at bedtime.
- Take a hot bath to relax.
- Don't worry if sleep doesn't come immediately. The average person takes about thirty minutes to fall asleep.
- If sleep is a problem at night, don't make up for it with daytime naps. (You'll never correct your sleeplessness that way.)
- Never go to bed angry with your spouse.

- Avoid drugs.
- Combine these tips with others mentioned in chapter 8—music, meditation, and deep breathing.

Toss out the Bathroom Scales

If you're gutsy enough to get rid of your alarm clock, why not really throw caution to the wind and toss out your bathroom scales too? At least that is the advice of Dr. Bryant Stamford, director of the Health, Prevention and Wellness Center at the University of Louisville School of Medicine. Weight fluctuations can be caused by so many factors—water retention, increased muscle mass, a decrease in activity—that a pound here or a pound there shouldn't be a source of concern. The best way to free yourself from daily weigh-ins is to eliminate the temptation—the scales. Occasional weight checking, perhaps on a weekly basis, is appropriate. Daily preoccupation with weight gain or loss is not.

Rather than going on a diet, it's smarter to fix the diet you're on. Three well-planned meals a day keep your energy level stable and fortify your body against the physical problems that often result from anxiety. Also, a trim physique does wonders for your self-concept.

Trendy diets that jolt a person's eating habits on a short-term basis do little to improve long-term lifestyles. Any weight *lost* is usually *found* as soon as more comfortable eating routines are reinstated. If you are dieting, keep in mind that you shouldn't lose more than about 1 percent of your existing body weight per week. For example, if you weigh 150 pounds, you should regulate your diet so that you lose about a pound and a half a week. You also will need to adjust your food intake downward as you age.

The best advice is old advice, but too few people follow it. Food should be chosen from the four basic food groups: milk, vegetable/fruit, meat, and bread/cereal. Most Americans eat far too much sugar and salt and way too many fatty foods. On the other hand, we usually don't eat enough fiber, fish, poultry, fresh fruits, and vegetables.

Often people wait until they have health problems to change

the way they eat. *After* they're diagnosed as having hypertension, they decrease their salt intake. *After* they suffer colitis, they learn the value of fiber. The truth is, the leading causes of death among Americans today are heart disease, cancer, high blood pressure, and stroke. Each of these illnesses is directly affected by lifestyle, and how well a person eats and how well he handles anxiety are key parts of his lifestyle.

Take a Break

When the twelve disciples of Jesus returned home after their first preaching and healing mission, Jesus listened to all their reports and then made a suggestion: "Come aside by yourselves to a deserted place and rest a while."[4] The kind of rest He prescribed for them was physical and mental, and it contained the same three components that are so valuable today in reducing anxiety and stress. These components are: a change of scene, a change of activity, and adequate time to rejuvenate.

It's important to note that Christ didn't merely suggest that they get a good night's sleep, and neither did he dismiss them with the old platitude, "You'll feel better in the morning." He clearly instructed them to leave their obligations behind, even though their work was far from complete, and retreat to a place that was remote and quiet. He knew they could never rest where they were, no matter how determined they might be. "For there were many coming and going, and they did not even have time to eat."[5]

Sound familiar?

The men were given a change of assignment to replenish their energy. Whereas they had been on their own in their new ministries, now they were back in a support mode. Much of their responsibility was eased as Jesus assumed the leadership role and preached to the thousands of people who trailed after them. The disciples were given tasks, but they were physical tasks: rowing the boat; getting the loaves and fish; telling the people to sit in groups on the grass.

The principles that Jesus practiced in this story are practiced today by organizations that recognize the value of breaking the work routine. Many companies not only offer their employees generous vacation benefits but also insist that the employees take advantage of the time off. Use it or lose it is the rule. In addition, organizations arrange employee picnics, distribute complimentary tickets to ball games, and encourage attendance at workshops and seminars on company time. Although money may be lost on such "nonproductive" activities, employees return to their desks rested, enthusiastic, and with more positive attitudes.

Individuals need to apply this principle on a personal level as well. Anxiety often is the outgrowth of boredom, so give yourself something better to do than to worry. Choose an activity that can be enjoyed regardless of the weather, and plan to indulge in it at least three times a week. The benefits are threefold:

- When you put your mind on something different, you give it a minivacation from its usual routine. Problems become "do-able" after you return to them refreshed.
- The activity and your enthusiasm for it will make you more interesting to the people around you (when you are bored, you're often boring).
- Your outside activity can boost your self-esteem.

This last point is best explained by a man who makes his living by helping others enjoy their hobbies. Doug Pratt is the special projects director for the Academy of Model Aeronautics in Reston, Virginia. Says Doug:

> I've always been fascinated by what people do in their spare time. It seems to me that we live in an age in which many people work at jobs they feel no pride in to keep the wolf from the door and food on the table. I know guys who tighten bolt A on every car that comes off a certain assembly line, but go home at night and build full-rigged models of the *Bounty* or radio-controlled airplanes. They have something they can point to that says, "I'm special. I did this."

Tennis, Anyone?

The final fitness factor each of us can control may be the most difficult of all: exercise. Some time-management whizzes combine the need for a hobby with the need for exercise, and they make golf, tennis, basketball, or jogging their favorite pastimes. They've discovered that you don't need to be a Steffi Graf or a Magic Johnson to benefit from a rigorous workout.

The Association of Fitness in Business once did a survey to determine why people exercise. Surprisingly, weight loss wasn't the most common answer. It placed second. More than 60 percent of the people who responded said they exercised to boost their spirits and to feel better. The third most popular answer, right after weight loss, was "to reduce stress" and, finally, "to boost energy level."

We recommend a minimum of twenty minutes of exercise three times a week. Too often people set a more demanding exercise schedule—an hour four days a week—and lose interest after two or three weeks. It's better to be realistic and stick with the regimen.

A regular exercise program will benefit you physically and psychologically. The heart, circulatory system, muscles, and lungs are stimulated and strengthened by exercise. Such positive results may require a great deal of time to become obvious. What often is noticed immediately is the feeling of well-being (you've heard of jogger's high) that you will experience because of the release of chemicals known as endorphins.

Certainly one of the most beneficial kinds of exercise is walking. In fact, a well-planned walking program can bring about the same results as jogging, swimming, or bicycling. It burns calories at a rate of about 350 an hour, suppresses the appetite, improves digestion, relieves stress, and increases alertness by strengthening the heart and lungs and by supplying more oxygen to the brain. Best of all, it can be enjoyed by nearly everyone and requires no special equipment, strength, or talent.

The Choice Is Yours

When God gave us our intricate and wonderful bodies to manage, He included a few challenges. We call them choices. Think of it this way: We are the only creatures who make conscious decisions about when, how, and how much to sleep, eat, play, and exercise.

Animals function by instinct. They sleep when they're tired, and they become active only after they are fully rested. They eat when their stomachs growl, and they stop eating when they're satisfied. They play when they feel playful, and they get their exercise as part of their battle to survive.

We, on the other hand, force ourselves into artificial patterns, interrupt our rest with blasts from a clock, defy nature by pushing ourselves to exhaustion, continue to eat even though we're no longer hungry, and refuse to make time for recreation and exercise. It's a wonder we survive as long as we do.

Managing a balanced lifestyle is a big responsibility. It comes down to choices. If we fail to make the right ones, we can work ourselves out of a job at an early age.

How Healthy Is *Your* Lifestyle?

Various factors determine your overall mental, physical, and spiritual health. Some can't be controlled such as your age, environment (pollution, weather, noise), genes, and gender (women have to beware of breast and cervical cancer while men are vulnerable to prostate problems). Fortunately, several factors are within your control. These include your habits, attitudes, sleep, stress level, diet, exercise, and recreation.

As you read the following fifteen statements, put a check mark by those that accurately describe you.

1. I am a nonsmoker.
2. I eat three meals a day (starting with breakfast).
3. I am within five pounds of my ideal weight.
4. I exercise for at least twenty minutes, three times a week.
5. I sleep from seven to eight hours a night.
6. I am satisfied with my physical appearance.
7. I set aside time for daily devotions.
8. I have several close friends whom I see/talk with regularly.
9. I am familiar with tension's warning signs and know techniques to reduce them.
10. I have indoor and outdoor hobbies that I enjoy often.
11. I am a nondrinker.
12. I avoid making too many major changes within a twelve-month period.

13. I am confident about my professional and social abilities.
14. I schedule regular vacations.
15. I wouldn't hesitate to see a counselor or therapist if my doctor recommended it.

There is no "passing" score for this quiz. Review the statements that you were unable to check. Consider integrating those statements into your list of personal goals.

10.

Self-Talk/Self-Concept

JUST WHO DO you think you are?

How you answer that question could determine how much anxiety you will suffer in your life. Anxiety and self-concept are closely related. We know this is true because the proof is in our practice. Think for a moment about the patients you have met so far in this book. In each case, the patient's self-concept was negative and inaccurate and proved to be the source of tremendous anxiety.

First there was Linda J. in chapter 1. She saw herself completely at fault for the failure of her marriage, her illness, and her inability to perform as the perfect mate for her not-so-perfect husband. For years she refused to recognize and use her many talents, but tried instead to be what she couldn't be—a submissive southern belle whose life revolved around the country club. Result? Anxiety.

Then there was Dr. Peter M. in chapter 4. While other people saw him as a brilliant surgeon, he perceived himself to be a failure and an embarrassment to his parents. He linked his worth to his work and tried every day to prove his ability by turning in a performance that would burn out Marcus Welby. He wouldn't admit it, but he was angry at himself and at his parents. He was mad enough to kill somebody, and he chose himself as his victim. That is anxiety at its most dangerous.

Cynthia Rowland, the witty, pretty, TV personality introduced in chapter 7, was convinced that her body was fat, ugly, and permanently damaged by a childhood accident. Nearly three months of hospitalization were necessary to break down her negative and inaccurate perception of herself and replace it with a realistic tolerance of her flaws and an honest appreciation of her gifts. Only then did her anxiety subside.

Linda J., Dr. Peter M., and Cynthia Rowland saw themselves in negative terms. To rid themselves of anxiety, they first had to change their negative self-images to positive self-images.

How each person views himself determines what kind of life he will have, what his actions will be, and whether he will be anxious or enjoy inner peace. We find examples of this not just in our files, but throughout history.

An excellent illustration of how negative self-concept caused a group of people to shun an opportunity and suffer anxiety and how positive self-concept spurred another group to action is found in the Old Testament when God told Moses to send spies into Canaan. The soldiers' assignment was to observe and report back to Moses on that country's people, land, and military strength. Should the Israelites attempt to claim the country for themselves? The answer hinged on what the spies saw (or what they *thought* they saw) while on their mission.

"The people living there are powerful, and their cities are fortified and very large; and what's more, we saw . . . giants there!" said the majority of the men who slipped into Canaan, then retreated to Moses' camp for a debriefing. "The land is full of warriors, the people are powerfully built, and we saw . . . descendants of the ancient race of giants. We felt like grasshoppers before them, they were so tall."[1]

Two other spies witnessed the same situation but reported it in a different way.

"It is a wonderful country ahead, and the Lord loves us," they enthused. "It is very fertile, a land 'flowing with milk and honey!' Oh, do not rebel against the Lord and do not fear the people of the land. For they are but bread for us to eat! The Lord is with us and he has removed his protection from them! Don't be afraid of them!"[2]

The reports to Moses differed because the first was issued by a group of soldiers who had a negative concept of their abilities and an inflated view of the abilities of others. They envisioned themselves as grasshoppers and the enemy as giants who could crush the helpless insects. The others spies maintained a positive self-concept, respected themselves, and were aware of the advantage they enjoyed by having the Lord solidly in their camp. Unfortunately, they were in the minority.

The anxiety of the negative soldiers soaked through the ranks and permeated the mass of Israelites. Their complaints were predictable. They couldn't sleep. They were depressed. They played "what if" games as they began to imagine the worst possible scenarios. They convinced themselves that Jehovah surely was going to kill them and make slaves of their wives and children. They looked around for someone to blame for what they perceived as their terrible predicament. Moses was the logical scapegoat, so they turned on him and threatened to replace him with another leader.

We make the same mistakes today and suffer the same consequences—lack of sleep, depression, and worry. We look around for eligible candidates to blame for our dilemmas, and we generally settle on a boss, a spouse, or another innocent victim.

The link between self-concept and anxiety is as present in our time as it was in the days of Moses. People who view themselves as failures look to the future and see only stumbling blocks and defeats. They expect to trip and fall because they have no confidence in their ability to soar and excel. They fret and wring their hands over the gloomy fate that awaits them. They worry about the future because they don't feel able to cope with it.

Of course today's examples of negative self-concept and anxiety don't involve a nation of people looking for a home. But they *do* involve individuals anticipating important changes and shirking from wonderful opportunities. Every crop of new college graduates, for instance, includes youths who suffer from poor self-concept. These people survey the job market, worry they're not prepared, and convince themselves that their resumes fall short of the competition's. Even if they are *lucky* enough to get a job (they always credit success to luck, not skill), they're not sure they are capable of doing the work. Again, they worry needlessly. Negative self-concept generally causes them to be eliminated long before the jobs are awarded. They become what they perceived themselves to be in the first place—failures.

Negative self-concept is marked by faulty vision. People who suffer low opinions of themselves are vulnerable to anxiety because of their inability to see themselves and their challenges clearly. They underestimate themselves while overestimating everything around them. Unless they change, they always will be grasshoppers in a world of giants.

A Second Antidote to Anxiety

If negative self-concept can cause anxiety, then positive self-concept can reduce (or even relieve) anxiety. Part of a counselor's job is to help patients see themselves in honest, positive terms.

Easier said than done, you say? You're right.

Some people—even practicing Christians—secretly blame God for what they believe to be their imperfections. When a young man says, "If I were only taller (stronger, quicker, more agile), I might qualify for an athletic scholarship to college," he really is saying, "God made a mistake when He designed my physique." When a young woman complains, "If I were only smarter (prettier, wiser, friendlier), I would be a lot more successful," she's not criticizing herself as much as the One responsible for fashioning her.

If these scenarios sound familiar, it is because the young man and woman are using defense mechanisms similar to those described in chapter 6. Remember, a defense mechanism is an automatic reaction to frustration. It's a way that our brains trick us to relieve anxiety. In the case of the young man and woman, the mechanism of blaming God lets them off the hook. It allows them to think they aren't responsible for their lack of success. It frees them from guilt and anxiety. God is at fault.

As Christian counselors we try to show patients how they are using defense mechanisms to ease anxiety. Then, after we strip away the mechanisms, we get the patient to look at what's underneath: the inferiority complex and the poor self-image. The young man and woman first need to develop a more honest and favorable view of themselves and an acceptance of themselves. Only then can they rid themselves of anxiety and not merely hide it. They need to thank God for designing them exactly as He did. They need to say, as in Psalm 139:

I will praise You, for I am fearfully and wonderfully made;
Marvelous are Your works,
And *that* my soul knows very well.
My frame was not hidden from You,
When I was made in secret,
And skillfully wrought in the lowest parts of the earth.
Your eyes saw my substance, being yet unformed.
And in Your book they all were written,
The days fashioned for me,
When as yet there were none of them.[3]

Who are we to pass judgment on God's work? Isn't it presumptuous of us to suggest "improvements" in His plan for us? Like David, we should celebrate our uniqueness and be grateful for each trait and talent. David was the youngest in his family, he was not as large as Saul or Goliath (he couldn't begin to put on Saul's armor!), and his oldest brother Eliab even called him a worthless, irresponsible youngster not fit to take on the giant. Yet David accepted himself, and throughout the biblical record of his life this balanced perspective of himself set him apart. In fact, in that famous incident between David and Goliath, we see three classic examples of self-esteem that often show up in our counseling offices today.

First, we see the arrogant Goliath who has an unusually high view of himself; second, we see the paranoid, self-effacing Saul who has a poor self-concept and cannot function effectively because of it; and finally we see the balanced, realistic self-concept of David, who ultimately was successful.

God never ordered us to love ourselves. He didn't have to because our self-love should come naturally with an understanding of our relationship to Him. Some Christians, however, are uncomfortable with this idea of self-love because they equate it with conceit and vanity. (We've all known self-centered people who spend so much time staring up at their perceived "halos" that they create a pain in the neck for all those around them!)

The kind of positive self-concept that God wants us to have is marked by clarity, honesty, and balance. Positive self-concept is rooted in a person's knowledge that he has value because he is part of the body of Christ. He knows he is worthy because he understands that the Son of God died for him. She knows she has a contribution to make because she's aware of the unique gifts the Father has provided for her to explore and expand. Thus, as the apostle Paul explained, he can "think of himself, not more highly than he should, but evaluate himself realistically . . ." based on his God-given relationship with Christ (Romans 12:3). At peace with who he is and what he is, he's ready for a worry-free future. That future will be bright not only for him and for her, but for everyone around them because people who love themselves can more easily love their neighbors in the same way.

Three Sources of Anxiety

Anxiety can be traced to three sources. First, it can be rooted in a lack of self-worth, which is the basis of most psychological problems. Second, its source can be a lack of intimacy with others, which includes friends, spouses, family members, and people on the job. Third, it can be traced to a lack of intimacy with God. This intimacy is rooted in a personal faith that comes about not by religious activity or an attempt to earn our salvation but by an acknowledgment that we are imperfect sinners who place our personal trust in Jesus Christ. This personal act of faith is followed by continued growth in fellowship, which takes place as we meditate on God's Word, as we enjoy relationships with other Christians, and as we pray. This is how we become intimate with God. Poor self-image complicates all three areas.[4]

Although it's possible to change a negative self-concept to a positive self-concept at any point in life, the longer the negativism has been in place, the greater the challenge to reverse it. Too many defense mechanisms, acquired over many years, hide true feelings to relieve anxiety.

In such cases, we counselors have our work cut out for us. In our sessions with a patient we generally pick up on negative self-image very quickly. The slow part is tracing it backwards as it winds through his adolescence to its source, somewhere in the early years. If we are to get rid of it, we can't merely sever it in the present, but must expose its roots. The way we do this is by probing the patient's key relationships. We ask him if his parents gave him adequate praise during his growing-up years, had unrealistic expectations and refused to recognize anything short of perfection (as was the case with Dr. Peter M.).

We try to determine if, as a child, the patient was encouraged to speak up and share feelings. Or, were the parents so busy with other obligations that the child learned to withdraw and not make waves. Cynthia Rowland felt her parents had enough worry without the addition of her problems. Before long, she unconsciously decided that she had very little of value to say. Linda J. wrestled with a similar set of circumstances. Linda's negative self-image was established when she grew up in a family that believed a little girl should be seen, not heard. This belief was reinforced by Linda's husband, who kept her in the background as a pretty prop in a family setting that he dominated.

Even after we expose a patient's negative self-image, our mission is only partly completed. Turning the negative into a positive requires time and work. One technique that we teach is self-talk, a simple but effective way of changing the way each of us views himself and his life.

Self-Talk Spoken Here

We've all heard the expression, "Talk is cheap." Dr. Jerry Tarver, who teaches speech writing to professionals across the country, would argue that talk is anything *but* cheap. As proof, he cites a public relations firm that once charged $50,000 for a single speech and then had the nerve to say the firm had lost money on the deal! While that astronomical figure may not be typical, Tarver says that the going rate for a twenty-minute speech written by a freelancer is about $1,500.[5] Based on these numbers, we agree with him: Talk is not cheap.

Of course the idea behind the old expression is not dollars and cents, but that words are unimportant in comparison to actions. People can talk about their good intentions, but until they act on those intentions, nothing is accomplished. Words alone are worthless.

Or are they? What this simplistic idea fails to take into account is that a person's actions are a direct result of a very special kind of "talk" known as self-talk. This continuous stream of communication determines what we do, what we say, and how we feel about ourselves and others. Self-talk influences our self-concept and therefore directly influences our anxiety level.

Research has indicated that most people speak at a rate of about 150 to 200 words a minute. However, we carry on internal dialogue with ourselves—self-talk—at a phenomenal rate of some 1,300 words per minute. How can we think that fast? Most thoughts are expressed in fragmented visual pictures, sentence snatches, and fleeting concepts.[6] These thoughts are a nonstop flow of commentary, questions, sorting out of ideas, and expressions of our belief systems.

To better understand the self-talk concept and how it relates to self-image and anxiety, let's look at an example. Let's focus on a situation that is becoming increasingly common in our society today. Let's tune in on a woman who is suddenly forced into the job market at age forty. The reason she is job-hunting is unimportant. It could be that she is divorced, widowed, or needs extra cash for her children's college expenses. What is important is how she reacts to the situation. If she has low self-esteem her self-talk might go something like this:

> *The best I can hope for is minimum wage. After all, I have no education or skills. Why was I so foolish as to drop out of college after a year and a half? I'll be lucky to get any job at all. No one in his right mind will want to hire a middle-aged woman who hasn't typed a letter since her high school business education class. . . .*

Pretty soon the negative self-talk gives way to anxiety symptoms. Every morning she wakes up with a queasy stomach, knowing that she has to make follow-up phone calls, study the classified help-wanted section, and be interviewed by another personnel director at another company. She develops a headache and uses it as an excuse to cancel the interview (defense mechanism). Feeling guilty about the cancellation, she becomes preoccupied and snaps at her teenage son for tracking mud on the kitchen floor. She realizes she has hurt his feelings and tries to apologize. More guilt.

Negative self-talk can lead to low self-esteem or reinforce a negative self-concept that has been present for years. Soon the woman doubts her ability to succeed in any area. She becomes more anxious, suffers more headaches, and eventually stops trying to find a job all together.

Positive self-talk can have the opposite effect. Here's the same situation but with different internal dialogue:

> *I may not have finished college, but I've had a lot more experience than most grads. All those years as a volunteer taught me how to motivate people to work as a team. I've also learned how to handle money and keep tax records. With all the people I've come in contact with in the community, surely several will give me good letters of recommendation. My family is grown, my health is excellent. . . .*

"As he thinks in his heart, so is he," Solomon says in Proverbs.[7] This truth has been repeated for generations and packaged in every possible form. One of the most humorous sequences in television's original Dick Van Dyke series had Dick's character, Rob Petry, dragging out of bed on a Saturday morning to turn off a blaring alarm clock. He looked at the time, 7:00 A.M., and tried to remember all the chores he was going to accomplish by getting up at that early hour. He yawned, let his sleepiness get the best of him, reset the alarm for 9:00 A.M., and went back to bed.

Seconds later, Rob's wife, Laura (Mary Tyler Moore), tiptoed in and set the clock ahead to 9:00 A.M. The alarm blasted, and Rob hopped out of bed, stretched luxuriously, dropped to the floor for a few pushups, then exclaimed to Laura how he really had needed the extra two hours of sleep and how great he felt because of them. He believed it was nine o'clock and was convinced he had rested an additional two hours. His body and mind responded accordingly. He was relaxed, rejuvenated, and ready to face those same chores that he had wanted to avoid minutes earlier.

Our minds control our actions, either for the good or for the bad. The apostle Paul tells us several times that we can change our lives by seizing control of our self-talk. He urges us to bring "every thought into captivity to the obedience of Christ."[8] In Philippians he tells us what to concentrate on: "Whatever things are true, whatever things are noble, whatever things are just, whatever things are pure, whatever things are lovely, whatever things are of good report, if there is any virtue and if there is anything praiseworthy—meditate on these things."[9]

It's not easy to change. People who have been steeped in negativism for several years can't expect to reverse these thought patterns overnight. If they have suffered from low self-esteem and anxiety for a long period of time, they must rid themselves of old habits before they can replace them with new. They can best accomplish this by first committing themselves to making the necessary changes. Many people complain about their lives but are unwilling to adjust their behavior to facilitate a change.

Secondly, people have to make a real effort to stifle all worry talk. This includes both internal and external negative communication. As best they can, people must squelch the urge to talk or think in negative terms. That does not mean that they should ignore topics of concern, but that they should face them with a positive point of view. Instead of saying, "I'll never be able to get a job," the middle-aged homemaker should say, "I'm going to look for ways to promote my strengths."

The apostle Paul, writing to the church in Philippi, points out that God both instructs us to stifle all worry talk and provides the enablement to do this through His presence in our lives.[10]

Finally, the people who are seeking to make a change in their lives should carry on as if the desired change has already taken place. Dr. David Stoop explained it well when he wrote, "You can live 'as if,' or you can live the 'what ifs.' The 'what ifs' place you in the world of worry and anxiety; the 'as ifs' place you in the world of faith and trust."[11]

Self-talk affects self-concept, and negative self-concept leads to anxiety. If anxiety is a problem, positive self-talk may be the solution. As a start, the most valuable piece of internal dialogue to repeat is this: "Change is possible."

11.

Friends in Need

CYNTHIA ROWLAND, WHOM you met in chapter 7, was full of surprises. Not only did her trim physique belie her enormous consumption of food, but her friendly facade hid her extremely lonesome lifestyle. Cynthia's bright smile and quick wit made her seem so approachable, yet she had erected an invisible privacy fence around herself years earlier, and she refused to let any friend slip past the barrier. She didn't like herself and assumed no one else would like her either. Besides, if she allowed even a small group of people to become close to her, those friends surely would learn about her awful binge/purge habit. She simply couldn't risk the resulting rejection.

Like Cynthia, the majority of patients whom we hospitalize for anxiety don't have any close friends. Sometimes they won't admit this, and they'll point to colleagues and associates as "proof" of their sociability. "Friends?" they'll ask us. "I've got a million of 'em." But when we describe true friendship—the kind that is an essential element in worry-free living, they generally concede theirs don't qualify. Not only do these patients lack meaningful friendships, but they also lack an understanding of friendship's important role in everyone's mental health.

Author Don Hawkins, who served as pastor to several midwestern and southern congregations, recalls a poignant illustration. Don says he once took a phone call from a man from another city, a man he had met only two or three times. The man obviously was upset and needed to share his problems with someone. Since Don is a trained listener, he was glad to serve as a sounding board. At the conclusion of the conversation, the man gratefully thanked Don for listening.

145

"You're just about the only good friend I have," he said.

Those words bothered Don far more than the problems that had been aired during their talk. At best, the two men were casual acquaintances who rarely saw each other and only spoke on the telephone a few times each year. Yet the troubled man viewed Don as his only good friend. Don later commented that the man might have had fewer problems and might have coped with them better if only he had had the benefit of a close, ongoing friendship with someone he could see on a regular basis.

Andrew M. Greeley, author of *The Friendship Game,* talked about the common ground of friendship in this way: "In friendship we say, 'You and I both love me and you and I both love you.'"[1] Unfortunately, too often a person cannot establish and enjoy friendship because he has no love for himself. Rather than accepting himself for who he is and choosing to seek God's best for himself (which is the essence of love), he views himself with disdain and is convinced that everyone else sees him in the same negative light. Cynthia Rowland was a good example of this. Not until she began accepting and even liking herself was she able to tear down the privacy fence that surrounded her and to allow a number of friends to enter.

Friendship and Anxiety

The topic of friendship is the perfect bridge to move us from our discussion of how to overcome anxiety (Part Two) to our look at how to prevent anxiety (Part Three). It is a likely transition because it is essential to both the process of overcoming worry and the process of preventing worry.

Jesus emphasized the importance of friendship when He was asked, toward the end of His ministry, which of the 629 commandments should be given top priority. He responded in this order: First, He said, you should love God with all your hearts; and second, you should love your neighbors as yourselves.

Both of these commandments have major implications in terms of anxiety. By relinquishing control and allowing God to run our lives, we are relieved of the stress of grappling for command.

We can relax, assume a more peaceful posture, and express our love by worshiping and thanking God for caring about us and providing for us.

But we also need people, and this leads us to the second commandment. When Jesus reached back into Old Testament law to remind us to love our neighbors as ourselves, He was talking about an unconditional kind of love for people that takes the form of friendship and encouragement. It's interesting to note that the biblical word for encouragement also can be translated as "counsel," and means "to call alongside to help." In our treatment of anxiety disorders at the Minirth-Meier clinics, we've found that patients respond best if they feel that we love and accept them unconditionally. Each of our staff members tries to create an environment of love during the one-to-one counseling sessions and in group therapy. The warmth and support that radiate from this kind of setting help patients feel comfortable as they open up and share more of themselves than they may have ever shared in the past.

The concept of friendship as encouragement and counsel can work on several levels. It can happen between two friends, between two peers, between someone older and someone younger, between someone wiser and someone with less experience, or between persons from different economic backgrounds. It can occur between a professional such as a pastor and his parishioner; a therapist and a client; or a team of professionals (psychiatrist, counselor, psychologist) and a patient.

On whatever level the process takes place, the human dynamics are the same. A great deal of listening, encouragement, and counseling transpires. The goal is the same: healing.

To better understand the levels of care available in the treatment of anxiety and to see how friendship fits into the healing process, let's use the analogy of a physical, rather than a mental, illness. Let's look at the various steps that can be taken toward wellness.

The first step is self-help. If you have a sore throat or the flu, you may choose to medicate yourself with aspirin, cough drops, and bed rest. The second step toward wellness may involve telling a friend your problem and asking for advice. A third level of care might be to visit a local pharmacist. Since he interacts with doctors and patients, he knows what viruses are being passed around the community and what kinds of over-the-counter medication might be most helpful. On a fourth level, you might call a doctor's office, describe your symptoms to a nurse, and hear her counsel. At the next level you may decide to make an appointment with a doctor for a one-to-one consultation. Finally, at the most serious level, you might enter a hospital and be cared for by a team of experts.

The treatment of anxiety can follow the same pattern. Often the second step, seeking the counsel and encouragement of a good friend, solves the problem and eliminates the need for additional steps. Anxiety disorders occur when people turn their emotions inward. If these emotions are aired in the loving environment of friendship, they diminish in importance and lose their potential harmfulness. The encouragement that is provided by close friends can boost the healing process and even prevent an illness from occurring in the first place. Authors Frank Minirth, Paul Meier, and Don Hawkins know this from first-hand experience.

Mutual Encouragers

Drs. Frank Minirth and Paul Meier still laugh over the unlikely circumstances of their first meeting. Both were medical students at the University of Arkansas, although neither knew the other until the fateful day they were paired as cadaver mates. The timing couldn't have been better. Frank recalls those tough medical school days this way:

> The courses were unbelievably hard and the students were unbelievably smart. I would study late into the night. I would study at the supper table. I would study on Friday night, all day Saturday, and all day Sunday. The long, long hours of study zapped my energy. My weight dropped from 130 to 120 pounds. I was working out every day with weights, trying to increase my stamina, as well as my size. Still, I continually felt exhausted. The diabetes fought back and I struggled with it. *I must get up just one more day,* I would tell myself morning after morning. I felt discouraged and wondered if I would ever be able to make it through medical school.[2]

Into that stressful setting walked Paul Meier. The two were assigned to the same cadaver class, a course neither was excited about taking. Perhaps because their last names began with M, perhaps because they happened to sit at the same laboratory table, or perhaps because God knew they could help each other, the young doctors were teamed as cadaver mates.

"During those rough days in medical school, we became mutual encouragers," remembers Frank. "We became close Christian friends. Together we would sit down and ask ourselves how we could have an effect for Christ in our lifetime."[3]

The friendship that began in the sterile setting of a laboratory grew over the years, and the two doctors, now business partners as well as close friends, still use each other as sounding boards. Their circle of friends has expanded, and Dr. Minirth puts such an emphasis on developing close friendships that he meets a goal of building one close relationship every two to three years. Regardless of how busy a day may be, time is always set aside for phone calls and visits with these friends. In fact, the doctors agree that the busier the day, the more they need the encouragement and counsel of friends. They estimate that anxiety can be cut in half merely by verbalizing it to a good listener.

Standing Invitation

No one knows better than Don Hawkins how difficult it is for a pastor to develop and maintain close friendships. Not only does a minister usually uproot and relocate several times during his ministry, but he's generally viewed as one who solves problems rather than suffers problems. Many pastors fear that if they share their anxiety with a friend, they will be viewed as vulnerable and not strong enough to supply spiritual leadership to a congregation. Also, some ministers worry that if they develop close friendships with some members of their church, their actions will be resented, and other members will accuse them of "playing favorites."

During Don's years as a pastor he recognized his personal need for friends. In each of their church assignments Don and his wife quickly identified people with whom they could relax, unwind, and be themselves. These special friends varied in age and income levels. The common denominator was that the friends welcomed the Hawkins family, didn't expect perfection of them, and provided them with a refreshing kind of environment that replenished the energy that was sometimes depleted by the obligations of a busy ministry.

A standing invitation for Sunday afternoon fellowship was extended without pressure to accept or decline. Whenever the Hawkins clan had no commitment after church, they would join their friends for a leisurely dinner. The traditional pastor/parishioner relationship was suspended for a few hours in the caring, comfortable atmosphere of friendship. Somehow the demands of Monday morning never seemed overwhelming after an afternoon of good conversation with caring friends.

As simple and basic as this kind of friendship may seem, it's becoming a rare commodity in our fast-paced society. The staff of the Minirth-Meier Clinic knows this not only from their daily interaction with patients, but also from the quick feedback we authors get from our broadcast counseling ministry. Recently we participated in a radio call-in program that focused on the topic of worry. The phone lines were jammed as people from all parts of the country wanted to share their experiences. Although the callers described different types of problems, we noted that they shared a common emotion: loneliness. Some were single parents who faced the challenges of childrearing without the loving relationship of a spouse. Other callers had accepted a career move and had not cultivated friendships in their new locales. Still others were so concerned about succeeding in the corporate world that they refused to allow themselves any social time with peers.

Perhaps the most disturbing call we received during that broadcast came from a young man who said he had once been hospitalized for manic depression. His doctor had prescribed medication (lithium) and had recommended regular outpatient counseling sessions with a therapist. However, the young man had decided to exercise what he called "control" over his illness, not to take the medication, and not to schedule the sessions.

"I feel great," he exuded. "I'm not anxious; I don't feel depressed; I'm sleeping all right, and I don't need anybody's help. I can take care of myself."

While we congratulated him on his feeling of wellness, we gently added a note of caution. We explained that a person's probability of having recurrent manic episodes is increased after he's stopped taking lithium. There are also possibilities of side effects to the medication that could create a short-term feeling of well-being. Finally, we told him that manic depressive illness has a stronger genetic component than normal depression.

"If it takes a hundred ounces of worry to make somebody severely depressed, it may only take thirty ounces of worry to get someone with manic depressive illness to experience a manic episode," Dr. Meier pointed out.

We emphasized that if the caller refused to see his doctor, he at least needed to take into his confidence one or two close friends and share with them his medical history.

"Explain what your symptoms have been in the past, and ask your friends to watch out for you," urged Dr. Minirth. "If you start to feel agitated or depressed, you may not notice it yourself, but your friends will pick up on the changes in your behavior. Trust them with the information about your illness, and listen to them if they advise you to get help."

Who Makes a Good Friend?

Not all friendships are healthy. Some actually can *cause* anxiety instead of relieve it. If you feel some doubt as to whether or not a relationship is positive, ask yourself this question: "Is this friendship developing me?" If the relationship is one-way, with one partner always giving and the other partner always receiving, the answer is probably no. If it is a dependency relationship in which one person feels slighted if she isn't in her friend's company every day, the answer is no. If it is a fair-weather relationship that withers when one of the partners endures a period of adversity, the answer is no. If it is an ego-boosting relationship in which one person merely strokes the ego of the other person without giving honest— even negative—feedback, the answer is no.

Just as happiness and forgiveness are choices, so is friendship. Each of us has to choose to develop friendships, and each of us must decide what kind of and how many friends we want. A few, well-chosen, deep friendships are generally more beneficial to us than a wide circle of superficial acquaintances.

The Book of Proverbs offers good advice on how to select friends. Perhaps the most important verse is the one that states, "He who walks with wise men will be wise, but the companion of fools will be destroyed."[4] Our friends influence us, and in a nurturing kind of two-way relationship each participant often takes on certain characteristics of the other. Friendships can change us for the better or for the worse. The person who frequently is in the company of a wise friend is likely to become wiser because of it. The person who surrounds himself with fools risks becoming a fool.

As we examine the traits that make a person a valuable friend, we need to remember that we should covet these traits in ourselves as well. Friendship is something we give as well as something we get. Among the most valued characteristics to look for in a friend and develop in ourselves are:

LOVE. The kind of love that exists among friends is identified in the Bible as *filas*. Unlike the strong bonding that unites a mother to her child or the erotic attraction that links a husband and wife, *filas* is a likemindedness or kindred spirit that causes one person to say to another, "We have a lot in common; I like being with you."

In the film *Shenandoah,* Jimmy Stewart is approached by a young man who wants to marry Stewart's daughter and who gathers enough nerve to approach the older man and ask for the girl's hand.

"Why do you want to marry her?" asks Stewart.

"Because I love her," replies the suitor.

"That's not important," grumbles the father. "Do you *like* her?"

The love between friends is based on common attitudes, not similar backgrounds, age, or financial status. One of the strongest friendships that is illustrated in the Bible is the relationship between

Paul and Timothy. In spite of age difference, the men share many of the same feelings and opinions. Timothy, much younger than Paul, benefits from Paul's wisdom and experience. Paul, on the other hand, relies on Timothy to replenish his zest for life when Paul is lonely, discouraged, and tired.

PEACE. At times the most valuable characteristic of a friend is his ability to listen quietly and be silent rather than critical. A peaceful person looks for ways to calm, not cause, strife. Often an effective antidote to anxiety is the willing ear of a friend. Such a friend doesn't judge what he hears, doesn't repeat what is said, and doesn't smother the troubled person with platitudes.

OPEN COMMUNICATION. A genuine friend isn't afraid of confrontation. It's human nature for all of us to gravitate to people who flatter us, but flattery is misleading and can cause us to continue negative behavior. Open communication is based on honest feedback and keeps us on track. Proverbs 27:6 warns that, "Faithful are the wounds of a friend, but the kisses of an enemy are deceitful."

The young man who contacted us on the radio broadcast and said he had cured his manic depression without drugs or therapy desperately needed a friend to monitor his behavior. In such situations, a friend can take on the familiar role of "sounding board." He can react to words and actions and keep the other on a healthy course.

MUTUAL IMPROVEMENT. Friends "bounce off" ideas on each other and depend on positive and negative responses to help them make decisions. The result of this give-and-take exchange is mutual improvement. The concept of iron sharpening iron—"As iron sharpens iron, so a man sharpens the countenance of his friend"[5]—is as true today as it was hundreds of years ago.

Dr. Paul Meier once counseled a man who had a driving desire for a speaking ministry. The gentleman was a committed Christian who wanted to touch other people's lives with stirring sermons. The problem was that he was a lackluster orator. Dr. Meier urged him to "test" his career aspirations on his friends. He did and was briefly dismayed at the response. It wasn't what he had wanted to hear, but it caused him to change his professional direction. The friends suggested that the man's true gift was motivating young people to know Jesus Christ. The man took additional seminary training, and today he is a successful minister of youth evangelism.

REFRESHMENT. Some people have the natural ability to spark a feeling of joy and lightness among friends. Proverbs 27:9 talks about the sweetness of a man's friend being similar to perfume and ointment. Paul said that Onesiphorus, an obscure friend of his, "often refreshed" him.[6] What better way could there be to relieve anxiety than to enjoy the company of someone who makes us smile and relax?

The Friendship Factor

An old expression claims that genuine friendship is like sound health; its value is seldom known until it is lost. We believe that friendship is not only similar to good health, but that it plays a key role in good health. For that reason, everyone who is prone to anxiety—and that includes most of us—should take time to develop and nurture genuine friendships.

In the next chapter we will look at ten proven ways to prevent anxiety from recurring. As effective as the ways are, they will even be more successful if they are part of an overall health program that includes the friendship factor.

How Good a Friend Are You?

Meaningful friendships are important but fragile relationships that can enhance good mental health and reduce negative anxiety. To *have* a good friend, you must *be* a good friend, one willing to devote time and effort to the relationship. The following true-false quiz will help determine how much you know about friendship.

1. Envy is a normal part of many friendships.   T   F
2. It's possible to have too many friends.   T   F

3. In selecting friends, you should look for people of similar   T   F
   age and with similar backgrounds.

4. It's more difficult to make friends now than twenty years   T   F
   ago.

5. It's possible to outgrow friends.   T   F

6. Friendships that are too strong can be harmful.   T   F

7. In our mobile society, long-term friendships are nearly   T   F
   impossible to sustain.

8. A male-female friendship is not always the first step   T   F
   toward romance, but can be a healthy sign of the times.

9. The best friendships are 50-50 kinds of relationships.   T   F

10. Some people find it very difficult to make friends.   T   F

1. True, but that doesn't mean it should cause the demise of the relationship. Be honest about it; admit to your friend that he has a talent or quality that you envy. Clear the air. Chances are he'll respond with a similar "confession."

2. True, if your purpose is merely to clutter your social calendar and keep yourself so busy that you escape solitude. Most people maintain friendships of different degrees. Friends range from pleasant acquaintances to intimate soulmates.

3. False. It's healthy to have friends who span the age brackets and who represent different socio-economic backgrounds. Acceptance is the key. For a friendship to flourish, friends must accept each other for what they are and not try to initiate changes.

4. True. Think of how our society has been altered in the last few decades: More women are in the workforce; life in the suburbs means longer commuting time and less socializing time; families are relocating more often; people are more security-minded and are installing fences and other "barriers"; the competitive nature of big business pits peers against each other in a survival-of-the-fittest kind of environment; working couples, tired at the end of the week, choose to withdraw and get away rather than seek the company of others.

5. True. Two women may be drawn together because they have children involved in the same activities. The women work on committees together, share carpool duties, and enjoy discussing their common interests. After the children are grown, the women find they have less and less to discuss. The relationship ends quietly and naturally.

6. True. It's possible to be too good a friend during a crisis and actually make an unhappy situation worse. This can happen in two ways. First, you can hover over a hurting friend and almost smother her with concern. Second, you can empathize with a hurting friend to the point of adding to her suffering. She feels as if she's inflicting pain by allowing you to share her hurt. By assuming her burden you try to lighten it, but the opposite occurs.

7. False. They merely require more work. Several ingenious methods can keep friendships alive and well. Cassette tapes can be recorded and swapped by mail; long-distance phone visits can take place on a set schedule in order to maintain regularity; same-time-next-year vacation reunions can be arranged at a geographic location convenient to both.

8. True. Many men and women are viewing each other as colleagues who share common interests and goals. No longer does a male-female relationship have to be based on romantic attractions. A man now feels less of a need to be macho with a female friend, and a woman doesn't try to be one of the boys.

9. True. A one-way friendship can be the source of great anxiety. An equal give-and-take friendship develops both partners.

10. True. If a person is to make friends easily he must project friendliness. This involves taking the risk of being rejected. Often persons who are preoccupied with themselves aren't willing to show their vulnerability to others.

12.

Worry-Free Living Is a Choice

ONE OF OUR favorite stories tells of an elderly man who immigrated to the United States several years ago from one of the Communist bloc countries of Eastern Europe. After his papers were processed he found his way to a New York cafeteria where he sat down and waited for someone to bring him a menu and take his order. No one came. Eventually a woman with a full tray of food approached, realized the old man's dilemma, and explained how American cafeterias work.

"Start at the beginning," she said kindly. "Look at all the choices that are available, decide what you want, and just reach out and take it. When you get to the end, you'll be told how much you must pay for the things that you've chosen."

The old man was a bit of an old-world philosopher, and it wasn't long after he had settled in his new home that he made this observation: "Life in America is a lot like that New York cafeteria," he mused. "The options are endless, but you'll never get what you want if you sit around and wait for someone to deliver it. Anything is possible—a job, an education, a home, a car—but you have to be willing to get up and go after it. And in the end, you have to pay the price of your choices."

We agree, but choices aren't limited by what country you live in, and they certainly extend beyond material items such as food, jobs, homes, and cars. They include emotions, both positive and negative. Anxiety is a choice. Worry-free living is its alternative. Which do you want? And are you willing to pay the price?

As the elderly man observed, wishing for something doesn't

assure that the something will be delivered. Each of us has to take the initiative, pursue the desire, and be accountable for the price. In the case of worry-free living, that price might include adhering to a balanced lifestyle, spending time in self-examination, nurturing strong friendships, recognizing and discarding defense mechanisms, engaging in positive self-talk, and even seeking professional care when self-help isn't enough.

The choices aren't always easy, and they sometimes involve sacrifice. When Don Hawkins, executive director of the Minirth-Meier Clinic, is invited to speak about our staff's treatment of anxiety, he often opens with an anecdote about a little boy whose fist became wedged in his mother's valuable antique flower vase.

"Mom, I can't get my hand out," said the youngster, nearly in tears.

The mother's anxiety matched her son's as she doggedly tried soaking the hand in warm water then swabbing petroleum jelly around the neck of the vase. No luck. She perspired, she gritted her teeth, and her voice became shrill as she scolded the boy for putting his hand into the vase in the first place. Her nervousness increased as she realized the inevitable: She was going to have to break the beautiful treasure to free her little boy's hand. She had no other option. Just as she was about to shatter the vase, the child looked up at her inquisitively.

"Mom, would it help if I let go of the penny?" he asked.

Choices. In the case of the little boy, there could only be one, but it wasn't a clear-cut, right and wrong, black or white decision. Vase or penny? The child could probably have mounted an argument for both sides. Choices often involve sacrifice.

In his book *When the Road Gets Rough,* our good friend and colleague Walt Bird outlined five choices all of us have when we're faced with anxiety. According to Walt, we can:

- *Curse the anxiety* that plagues us. This may seem to be the tough-line approach, but too often it results in feelings of anger and resentment toward God.
- *Nurse the anxiety.* Over a period of time this will only produce self-pity and the familiar "Why me, Lord?" questions.
- *Rehearse the anxiety.* Practice makes perfect, and we can

easily become professional worriers if we cling to anxiety in an attempt to wring sympathy from others.

- *Disperse the anxiety.* A fine line exists between using friends as sounding boards and taking advantage of them as dumping grounds. Heaping our problems on others isn't fair. It might lighten our load, but it only adds to the burden of the people closest to us. Besides, dispersing anxiety doesn't make the worry go away; it merely spreads it around.

- *Reverse anxious thoughts.* By practicing positive self-talk techniques as explained in chapter 11, we can learn to view problems as projects that can be completed successfully. All that is required is a realization of the gifts God gave us and a willingness to apply those gifts to finding solutions.[1]

Just as no waitress came over to the old man in the cafeteria and asked him what he wanted, God doesn't take our order and dutifully deliver it to us. Instead, he equips us with the intelligence to make good decisions and the ability to reach out for those things we decide are right for us. Penny or vase? Which will it be? The little boy couldn't have both.

Anxiety or worry-free living? What do you prefer? It all comes down to choices: curse, nurse, rehearse, disperse, or reverse anxiety.

In Search of Inner Peace

Although the mission of this book has been to accomplish two goals—to teach you how to overcome anxiety and to show you how to prevent it from recurring, it never promised to be a cure-all. As you implement the suggestions we've offered in these pages, you may be discouraged by two truths. First, achieving worry-free living is no easy task. And second, even if you attain it, there is no guarantee that you'll be able to sustain it permanently.

In Proverbs, God gives us His blueprint for anxiety-free living when He urges us to be wise and to develop good judgment and common sense. Much of the advice we've shared in this book involves good judgment and is based on common sense. By making wise decisions, God says, each of us can have not only a long life but a happy one, too. In such a life we won't slip or fall; we will run instead.

But first things first. God tells us that a determination to be wise is the first step toward becoming wise.[2] Likewise, a determination to be free of worry is the first step toward worry-free living. Even after we've taken that step, we're not done. We then need to design and follow a plan to achieve our goal. "Watch your step, stick to the path, don't sidetrack, and be safe," God says. This book has attempted to show you the path; now it's up to you to stick to it.

Becoming sidetracked in the quest for worry-free living is common. We know this firsthand. Each of us has chosen worry-free living over anxiety, and each has designed a plan to achieve his goal. We meditate, we pray, we memorize Scripture, we maintain a balanced lifestyle, we have strong friendships, we live one day at a time . . . and, yes, each of us has become sidetracked from time to time.

When Paul Meier decided to shake loose of anxiety by changing his workaholic lifestyle, more than three years were required before he was truly successful. Looking back, he likens those early efforts to learning how to ride a bicycle. At first he had to concentrate totally on what he was trying to do. His natural tendency was to become overly involved in activities; to counter this inclination he had to constantly remind himself of the path he was trying to follow. In time, he replaced old behavior patterns with new ones, and a lighter workload became the norm. Now he doesn't have to work as hard to assure his anxiety-free life. It's been established and now only needs to be maintained.

Don Hawkins still runs through airports O. J. Simpson style, but now tries to limit his travels to one or two trips per month. Knowing the pitfalls of his Type A personality, he compresses all his out-of-town business meetings into one or two days. He then arranges a flight plan that will take him to airport terminals or seminar sites for meetings, then on to the next stop on his circuit, and ultimately back home. This packed, efficient approach to travel allows him to spend an abundance of quality time with his family, yet utilize ministry opportunities and take care of business responsibilities.

Any time that Frank Minirth is tempted to become sidetracked, he recalls his second year of medical school when he suffered a serious case of sophomore syndrome that put him back on track. Frank maintains that every med student succumbs to the condition sooner or later. It merely means that the student becomes convinced that he has whatever disease he happens to be studying. The future doctor reads about the symptoms, and he experiences them. If the prognosis is grim, he starts believing his days are numbered.

Unfortunately, when Frank began researching diabetes for a class, he didn't imagine he had the disease; he already knew he had it. The textbook was far from upbeat in its assessment of the condition. All the possibilities, including early death, were outlined in painful detail. Frank, who had eased off his physical fitness program because of the demands of school, was jolted by the realization that his becoming sidetracked could have serious repercussions. He immediately revived his jogging schedule, adhered to his weight-lifting regimen, and paid meticulous attention to his diet and rest habits. Self-improvement became a goal. He even enrolled in a speech therapy class to overcome a slight speaking impediment he had experienced since childhood. Today, not only is he the picture of vibrant health, but he also is the primary speaker on a radio and television series.

Grab an Oar

At the Minirth-Meier Clinic, our staff applies this advice to a lot of the anxiety problems we see: *If you find yourself in a rowboat during a storm, you should pray hard and row to shore.* The advice is reminiscent of the old man in the cafeteria who learned he had first to determine what he wanted, then to reach out and claim it. And it echoes the advice of Proverbs that everyone has the responsibility to choose a path and to follow it.

Worry-free living is attainable if you're willing to pray hard and work toward your goal. How hard and how long you must work will depend on how far away from shore you are when you begin. Success *can be achieved* because all things are possible through Jesus Christ.

Just grab an oar.

APPENDIX

INTRODUCTION TO APPENDICES

THE DETAILS IN the appendices that follow are provided for several reasons.

First, the text of this book was written for the general public. Yet, there are those who want in-depth information in specific areas (medical, psychological, theological).

Second, these appendices are written because anxiety is so widespread and of such importance. Over twenty million Americans have a psychophysiological disease in which anxiety is a major factor. In fact, anxiety disorders are the leading category of all the types of psychological disorders. It seems that the twentieth century is more anxiety ridden than any other era in history.

Third, the appendices are provided because we believe a balanced, comprehensive approach is needed in dealing with anxiety, based on the biblical perspective on the "whole [person], spirit and soul and body" (1 Thess. 5:23). We trust that details of the biochemical, physiologic, neurologic, hormonal, immune, psychological, and theological aspects will help explain the need for such a balanced, comprehensive approach. We cannot focus only on the medical or only the spiritual or only the psychological. Each part affects the other.

Christian psychiatry can and should provide the balance to deal with all. To avoid the medical (brain neurotransmitters, hormones, autonomics, nervous system, psychophysiologic disease, immune system, and others) is to doom some to a nonfunctional or psychotic life, perhaps even to death. To lift psychology above Scripture is even more dangerous. To do this is to lose sight of eternal destiny. Our standard of authority, the Bible, says that man is basically selfish (Jer. 17:9) and that only through Christ is there ultimately hope.

We can benefit from psychology, realizing that nothing is "new under the sun" (Eccles. 1:9). Our approach recognizes the Bible as foundational and supreme (Deut. 32:46–47, Josh. 1:8, Psalm 1:2–3, Jer. 15:16, Is. 39:8, Is. 55:11, Matt. 24:35). Of course, apparent scientific truth should never be elevated to the degree of divine truth as revealed in Scripture. Yet we also use scientific knowledge as, in fact, we all do every day. If we use these principles in our approach, Christian psychiatry can provide significant help in overcoming anxiety medically, psychologically, and spiritually.

APPENDIX 1

GUIDELINES FOR "FIGHTING FAIR"

THE *WAY* A conflict is resolved often is more important than the resolution itself. *How* decisions are made sometimes has a more lasting effect on participants than the decisions have. If confrontations are badly handled, a key player can suffer personality and self-concept wounds that are difficult to heal. Such key players include not only the persons who are directly involved in the disagreement, but observers as well, particularly children.

The following twenty guidelines offer rules for fighting fair. Although originally designed for husbands and wives, they are equally applicable to any relationship. The word *partners* indicates persons involved in the conflict.

1. Consider your relationship a long-term commitment, not to be discarded because of one disagreement, no matter how serious it may be.

2. Agree always to listen to each other's feelings, even if you consider those feelings inappropriate.

3. Commit yourselves to both honesty and acceptance.

4. Determine to attempt to care for each other unconditionally, with each partner assuming 100 percent of the responsibility for resolving the conflict (a 50/50 concept seldom works).

5. Consider all the factors in a conflict before bringing up the conflict to your partner.

6. Limit the conflict to the here and now. Never bring up past failures, since all past failures should already have been forgiven.

7. Eliminate the following phrases from your vocabulary:
   A. "You never" or "You always."
   B. "I can't" (always substitute "I won't").
   C. "I'll try" (usually this means "I'll make a half-hearted effort but won't quite succeed").
   D. "You should" or "You shouldn't" (these are parent-to-child statements).

8. Limit the discussion to the one issue that is the center of the conflict.

9. Focus on that issue rather than attacking each other.

10. Offer your partner some time to think about the conflict before discussing it (but never put it off overnight).

11. Each partner should use "I feel . . ." messages in expressing a response to whatever words or behavior aroused the conflict. For example, "I feel angry toward you for coming home late without calling me first" is an adult-to-adult message that is appropriate between spouses, whereas "You should always call me

167

when you're going to be late for supper" is a parent-to-child message. Such an "order" causes the mate to become defensive.

12. Never say anything derogatory about your partner's personality. Proverbs 11:12 (TLB) tells us, "To quarrel with a neighbor is foolish; a man with good sense holds his tongue."

13. Even though your partner won't always be right, consider him or her an instrument of God, working in your life.

14. Never counterattack, even if your partner does not follow these guidelines.

15. Don't tell your partner why you think he or she does whatever it is (unless you are asked), but rather stick to how you feel about what is done.

16. Don't try to read your partner's mind. If you're not sure what was meant by something said, ask for clarification.

17. Be honest about your true emotions, but keep them under control. Proverbs 15:18 (TLB) reminds us, "A quick-tempered man starts fights; a cool-tempered man tries to stop them."

18. Remember that the resolution of the conflict is what is important, not who wins or loses. If the conflict is resolved, you both win. You're on the same team, not opposing, competing teams.

19. Agree with each other on what topics are out of bounds because they are too hurtful or have already been discussed (bad habits, continued obesity, time-consuming hobbies, and so on).

20. Pray about each conflict before discussing it with your partner.[1]

APPENDIX 2

DEFENSE MECHANISMS

IN CHAPTER 6, "The Coverups," we discussed several of the most common psychological defense mechanisms that people use to ease and avoid anxiety. Many more exist. Listed below are several additional techniques that the human brain has devised to avoid the truth. A quick definition follows each entry.[1]

Distortion—Persons reshape their external reality to suit their inner needs. Often distortions involve grandiose delusions and hallucinations such as hearing voices that no one else can hear.

Schizoid Fantasy—Persons find reality so painful that they escape through excessive daydreaming.

Isolation—A favorite of compulsive people who have very strict consciences, this mechanism allows unacceptable emotions such as lust or greed to be split off from conscious thoughts.

Repression—This is the primary defense mechanism on which all others are based. Unacceptable feelings and ideas are banished from conscious awareness.

Unhealthy Suppression—Persons continually postpone dealing with a conscious conflict. They promise themselves they will deal with the problem later, but later never comes.

Phariseeism—Persons become increasingly self-righteous and think they are better than others because of what they do or don't do religiously. Their motivation is to avoid becoming aware of their own shortcomings.

Defensive Devaluation—Persons criticize others as a way of convincing themselves that they are better than others. Unconscious inferiority feelings are covered.

Passive-Aggressive Unconscious Behavior—Persons who have repressed hostility toward some authority figure "get even" in a nonverbal, passive way such as pouting, procrastinating, acting inefficiently, or by being stubborn.

Withdrawal—Persons who tend to be introverted deceive themselves about an anxiety-producing conflict by physically removing themselves from the situation.

Displacement—Persons transfer an emotion from its original object to a more acceptable substitute. (They punch a pillow or hug a teddy bear.)

Regression—Persons faced with current conflicts return to an earlier point of emotional immaturity when they felt more protected from stress.

Sarcasm—Persons with suppressed hostility toward themselves or someone else ventilate that hostility without being aware of its existence by making critical jokes about themselves or others.

APPENDIX 3

THE COMPLEXITY OF ANXIETY

The Many Faces of Anxiety

ANXIETY COULD BE defined as a subjective emotion characterized by feelings of apprehension, dread, uneasiness, worry, and concern. It is an unpleasant anticipation of some kind of misfortune, danger, or doom. The symptoms of anxiety are varied and, at times, hard to recognize. Some individuals complain of "tension headaches," quivering voice, backache, sighing respirations, numbness, foul taste in mouth, butterflies in stomach, painful urination, impotence or frigidity, interference with coordination, interference with judgment, changes in activity, interference with efficiency and effectiveness and mental functioning, weakness, fatigue, cold hands or feet, tingling, blurring of vision, ears ringing, impaired relationships with friends or family, intense dreams.

Physical Symptoms of Anxiety

These include physical cardiovascular symptoms (chest pain, pounding heart, increased blood pressure, rapid heart beat); respiratory symptoms (dizziness, lightheadedness, labored breathing, hyperventilation, sense of choking or smothering, shortness of breath, lump in throat); musculoskeletal symptoms (eyelid twitching, fidgeting, muscle aches, muscle tension, tightness in chest, chest pain, tremor); gastrointestinal symptoms (anorexia, dry mouth, diarrhea, nausea, vomiting, stomach pain, painful swallowing, nervous stomach); genitourinary symptoms (frequent urination); dermatologic symptoms (clammy hands, flushing, pallor, sweating).

Behavioral Symptoms

Behavioral and physiologic manifestations include: hyperalertness, irritability, uncertainty, tense posture, overdependence, apprehension, impaired concentration, poor memory, distraction, jumpiness or being on edge, impatience, inability to sleep or fall asleep, startled reactions, talking too much, sexual interest and functioning impaired. Behavioral symptoms may also include an immediate need to escape from the current situation and development of avoidance behavior.

Cognitive Symptoms

Cognitive symptoms include fear of dying, going crazy, losing one's mind, losing control, fainting, embarrassment. Delusions and hallucinations can result but are rare.

Psychological Symptoms

In addition to the many physical symptoms described above, anxiety is a component of almost all psychiatric disorders (neurosis, psychosis, psychophysiologic disorders). In the neurotic disorders, the diagnosis is made on how the anxiety is handled. If the anxiety is left free-floating with symptoms as described above, generalized anxiety disorder exists. If the anxiety is displaced to a neutral object (dogs, elevators, airplanes, and so on), a phobia exists. If the anxiety is displaced to an ego alien thought or compulsive action, an obsessive-compulsive anxiety disorder exists.

Spiritual Confusion

Confusion may arise in the spiritual realm. Did a client really not trust Christ, or is he obsessing over it? Did a client really trust Christ, or did he just have an anxiety experience with hyperventilation? Did "faith healing" take place, or was it a conversion disorder? Did an altered state of consciousness take place, or was it a dissociative disorder? Did one have an out-of-body experience, or was it depersonalization?

Organic Disease

Confusion also arises in the medical area. Medical disease can produce what appears to be anxiety: tremors as pheochromocytoma of the adrenal gland, mitral-valve prolapse of the heart, hyperthyroidism, electrolyte abnormalities, hypoglycemia, ear disease, basilar-artery disease. Caffeine can produce anxiety-like symptoms. Many drugs, both illegal and prescription, can produce anxiety symptoms. Alcohol withdrawal produces intense anxiety symptoms. Temporal lobe epilepsy can produce what appears to be anxiety and hypereloquisity. Other neurologic diseases may have anxiety as a component: Huntington's disease, Parkinson's disease, Wilson's disease, multiple sclerosis, brain tumor, central nervous system infections, systemic lupus erythematosis (SLE), and porphyria. In summary, medical disease can produce what appears to be psychological anxiety, but in our experience the psychological cause is much more common.

Psychophysiologic Disease

Anxiety has long been considered a major factor in psychophysiologic disorders. What has not been realized is the degree to which anxiety plays a part in the production of medical disease.

Illnesses in which anxiety is often thought to play a significant role include: muscle contraction headache, migraine, obesity, anorexia nervosa, peptic ulcer, irritable bowel syndrome, ulcerative colitis, essential hypertension, thyroid hormone disturbance, disturbance in stability of diabetes mellitus, asthma, dermatologic or skin disorders such as rash, psychosomatic aspects of obstetrics and gynecology as in premenstrual syndrome, sexual dysfunction, and chronic pain.

Biochemistry and Memory in Anxiety Response

The neurology, physiology, and biochemistry combine to shape life responses. An event that occurs is picked up by the sensory receptors in the retina of the eye. The information is taken to the cortex and limbic parts of the brain. The brain contains billions of nerve cells, each with stored memory and each cell interacting with thousands of others. Sometimes verbal messages are stored. Sometimes feelings are stored. Sometimes both are stored. Sometimes only a visual or perceptual impression is stored. The circuits go back and forth millions of times in the twinkling of an eye to search for what in its past is most closely related to this event and what response should be forthcoming. Even in reading this material, not only is the brain searching for parallels with the past, but it is actually reprogramming for the future with the new data it is receiving. The biochemical recording will never be exactly the same again. And the system becomes even more complicated as the cortex (thinking) and the limbic (emotional) parts of the brain interact.

Anatomy of the Fear Response

The whole brain is involved in the anxiety response, but perhaps the most important parts are the hypothalamus and the amygdala nucleus. Lesions in these areas in animals produce dramatic alteration in the fear response. Stimulation of these areas produces intense fear. The neurotransmitters (especially GABA-Gamma-Aminobuttric acid) also play a significant role, as does an area of the lower brain stem (pons) known as the *locus coeruleus.* The reticular activating system of the brain also comes into play. Finally, some individuals are more prone to an anxiety response physiologically than others, as is seen in studies which show sodium lactate to trigger an anxiety attack.

A decision is reached and one or several results come forth.

Seven Responses to Anxiety

Healthy Choices

First, through the somatic and autonomic nervous systems the body is prepared for fight or flight. However, if the sufferer chooses wisely, no pathology results.

Psychophysiologic Disease

Second, the anxiety may affect the hypothalamus, which affects the autonomic nervous system, which picks out a genetically weak organ in which a psychophysiologic disease results over time (ulcer, high blood pressure, colitis, coronary artery disease, or others). Internal medicine or surgery often will be needed. Few would argue with treating here from a spiritual standpoint.

Anxiety may affect the neurotransmitters that are so important not only in anxiety disorders but in depressive and psychotic disorders as well. These neurotransmitters exist in the synapse between every two brain cells, and there are probably about 100 billion brain cells. If anxiety alters dopamine, the individual becomes psychotic. If anxiety affects serotonin, the individual becomes depressed. If anxiety affects norepinephrine, the individual becomes either depressed or manic. GABA is the neurotransmitter most likely important in the anxiety response. Endorphins and enkephalin may be involved in pain and pleasure.

Some Christians argue against treating these problems. We say that treatment is as necessary as dealing with the underlying psychological and spiritual issues.

Medical Disease

Third, the anxiety may affect the hypothalamus, which then affects the pituitary gland with all of its hormones (TSH, FSH, LH, ACTH, GH, prolactin, ADH, oxylocin) and the various endocrine glands. Medical disease may again develop. For example, if under anxiety ACTH is increased, then cortisol is altered and the immune system is altered, decreasing the B-lymphocytes that produce antibodies. With the immune system thus impaired, the individual is susceptible to bacterial and viral diseases. As virus may be one factor in some types of cancer, this may explain why people under stress seem more cancer-prone.

Life stress studies reveal that anxiety seems to predispose to illness in general. The speed of recovery from infectious disease and from surgical procedures is correlated with a person's lifestyle and exposure to anxiety. Type A individuals (aggressive, anxious, time urgent) are clearly more prone to heart disease. Research shows that anxiety associated with loneliness may be an important factor in both coronary artery disease and certain forms of cancer. If anxiety does not directly lead to disease, it may very well result in behavior that does. For example, tobacco use may account for one fifth of all deaths in America. Anxiety may lead to sexual sin in an attempt to overcome insecurity. The sexual sin may lead to AIDS—one of the biggest fears of this century. In short, anxiety kills.

Defense Mechanisms

Some individuals do not develop a medical disease, but their response to anxiety is to increase their use of defense mechanisms (ways they lie to themselves) and accentuate their personality traits.

For example, they may use projection to blame others, introjection to overly blame themselves, denial to avoid the truth, rationalization to justify sinful behavior, fantasy to escape, isolation to avoid an unwanted insight, passive-aggressive behavior or sarcasm to get even, displacement to a less threatening object, idealization of others for support, somatization to worry over the body rather than the real issue, and so on (see detailed list of defense mechanisms in Appendix 2).

Personality Accentuation

Likewise, basic personalities may become accentuated. The obsessive may become more rigid and controlling. The hysteric may become more emotional and act out sexually. The paranoid may become more suspicious; the borderline, more unstable; the narcissist, more self-centered; the cyclothymic, more depressed or high; the explosive, more given to temper outbursts; the sociopathic, more selfish; the passive-dependent, more dependent; the passive-aggressive, more passive and ineffectual; the schizoid, more withdrawn; the avoidant, more alone; the schizotypal, more odd; the dysthymic, more depressed.

Mental Manifestations

The individual may deal with the anxiety by developing mental symptoms that impair his occupational and social functioning over time.

If the symptoms are bizarre with a loss of touch with reality, the person has a *psychosis*—most likely, schizophrenia characterized by a flat affect, loose associations, ambivalence, being autistic, and having hallucinations and delusions. He may have escaped the anxiety by psychologically escaping reality (there is also a medical aspect, as noted above).

If the symptoms are psychological and affecting his functioning over time, he has, by definition, a *neurosis*. An affective disorder is characterized by the anxiety turned inward or *depression*. If the anxiety is generalized, he has a *generalized anxiety disorder*. If the anxiety is displaced to a neutral object, he has a *phobia*—acrophobia (high places), algophobia (pain), astraphobia (storms), claustrophobia (closed places), hematophobia (blood), monophobia (being alone), mysophobia (germs), nyctophobia (darkness), ocholophobia (crowds), pathophobia (disease), pyrophobia (fire), syphilophobia (syphilis), zoophobia (particular animal). *Agoraphobia* has received a lot of attention. It is the fear and avoidance of being in a crowd or in a public place from which escape would be difficult. This leads to increasing constriction of daily activities. If the phobia has to do with the avoidance of certain social situations, it is called a social phobia. If the individual has intense, overwhelming anxiety attacks with labored breathing, rapid heartbeat, chest discomfort, choking, dizziness, feelings of unreality, tingling in hands or feet, hot flashes, sweating, faintness, tremor, fear of dying or going crazy, he has a *panic disorder*. If he has anxiety symptoms associated with a recognizable stressor and intrusive recollecting of the event with recurrent dreams and diminished interest in life with sleep disturbance and hyperalert traits, he has a *posttraumatic stress disorder*. If he deals with the anxiety by going into an altered state of consciousness (multiple personality, fugue state, amnesia), he has a *dissociative disorder*. If he deals with his anxiety by the loss of control of a voluntary part of his body (blind, paralyzed, etc., but without physical pathology), he has a *conversion disorder*. He may deal with his anxiety by *depersonalization* or out-of-body feelings. He may deal with it by an overconcern and fear of disease—*hypochondriacal*. He may develop *somatization disorder* with many body aches and pains.

The preceding perspective on anxiety disorders leads to the observation of three levels of anxiety. For example, the obsessive-compulsive who fears he has committed the unpardonable sin has a true theological anxiety (A3) over the fear of spending eternity in hell. He also has usually some current day anxiety (A2) issues (we have most often seen rejection issues from friends or family). Finally, he usually has some deep anxiety feelings from childhood—unmet dependency needs, rejection, etc. (A1). The current day situation (A2) was close enough to the original memories and anxiety (A1) for the brain to produce an anxiety response which was promptly dealt with by displacing it to the worry over the unpardonable sin (A3). In therapy all three levels of anxiety must be dealt with—his fear of unpardonable sin through spiritual instruction, his current conflicts through present-day problem solving, and his deep hurts through insight and feeling resolution. (See Appendix 4: Treatment Approaches, for details.)

These psychological disorders also have a medical and spiritual component.

For example, consider obsessive-compulsive disorder of an individual who doubts his salvation. There is a spiritual problem, although it is not what the individual thinks. He clearly understood the Gospel and trusted Christ as a youth so that is not the issue. His spiritual problem is actually unresolved bitterness toward his father. The problem is spiritual in the sense that in a neurosis a person becomes self-centered, not Christ-centered. The problem is also psychological. Rather than look at his bitterness he uses his defenses of repression and isolation and focuses in on the obsession (rather than the true problem). The problem is also medical. PET scans show that metabolism of glucose in the brain is altered in such individuals. It is as though a record player becomes stuck on one groove. The circuits of the brain are jammed. This may be related to a seratonin imbalance, and medicine (Prozac) designed to alter that neurotransmitter may help.

Sinful Behavior

The individual may deal with the anxiety by turning to sinful behavior (see 1 John 2:15–17), which then produces added anxiety. He may turn to lust of the flesh (sex, alcohol, drugs, food). He may turn to lust of the eyes (materialism). He may turn to the pride of life (control, prestige, pride).

Diagnosing Anxiety

Anxiety is at times easy to recognize and at other times very difficult to spot. The most common method to diagnose anxiety is based upon the symptoms listed above. The patient lists his symptoms, and it is the counselor's job, based on his *clinical impression,* to diagnose the anxiety disorder. A second method of diagnosing anxiety disorders would have to do with *objective tests.* The MMPI (Minnesota Multiphasic Personality Inventory) test has been used for years to help in the diagnosis of mental disorders, including those of anxiety. An anxious individual would score high on scales such as D for depression and PT for psychosthenic. An anxious individual may in fact score high on several other MMPI scales. The MMPI is the most widely used psychological test in the world and, in general, is very objective. It is ordinarily used by licensed psychologists. Other psychological tests have also been used. There are projective type tests such as TAT (Thematic Apperception Test) and Rorschach Test. In these projective tests, the individual may very well project his anxiety onto pictures or whatever object is held in front of him. There are less sophisticated tests such as the Taylor Johnson Temperament Analysis (TJTA), which will also pick up on anxiety and is available for pastors. The Bender Gestalt Visual Motor Integration Test is used more for organicity, but may also show anxiety. Even the Draw-A-Person (DAP) Test may reflect areas of deepseated anxiety and insecurity.

Finally, *medical tests* are also used to diagnose mental disorders. These tests have been used more with depression than with anxiety, but there is an overlap. Some of the tests that have been used include the computerized tomography (CT) scan and Magnetic Resonance Imaging (MRI), which are like sophisticated x-rays of the brain. "CAT" scans and MRI scans have not proven helpful in diagnosing anxiety disorders. Of course, any structural change which may be seen, for example, in a schizophrenic brain which might have enlarged ventricles, would be picked up by these tests. Another advanced test called Positron Emission Transaxial Tomography (PETT) now permits an exciting way to look at the local activity of the brain which was formerly inaccessible. Biochemical processes such as glucose metabolism can actually be followed. A compound is labeled with a positron-emitting radionucleotide, and its metabolism can be followed in the brain. Individuals with obsessive-compulsive anxiety disorder seem to metabolize glucose more rapidly than is ordinary in the frontal lobe of the brain. The implication is that there is not only much physical activity taking place, but a great deal of psychological activity as well. In other words, anxiety is draining. For the most part, however, these sophisticated techniques do not yield significant insight into anxiety at this time. Other blood tests such as Dexamethazone Suppression Test (DST) are more useful in diagnosing depression, though it does seem that brain chemistry is also altered in anxious individuals. The Thyroid Releasing Hormone (TRH) and Rapid Eye Movement (REM) tests have also been used but found more useful in diagnosing depression. Further knowledge lies just around the corner for the anxiety disorders.

Anxiety disorders are sometimes obvious, but at other times they are not. The best way to diagnose these disorders lies in the clinician's clinical impression. Research may very well hold keys for the future in intense anxiety disorders as anxiety's affects on the body begin to emerge.

APPENDIX 4

TREATMENT APPROACHES FOR ANXIETY

IN THIS BOOK we have tried to differentiate anxiety from its close cousin: fear. But when we discuss treatment here we will often use the terms interchangeably. It is our goal that knowledge of these treatment approaches will point individuals to experience worry-free living.

Spiritual, Physical, and Psychological Issues

Our treatment approaches will reflect our understanding of the causes. Certainly, spiritual issues are of utmost importance and are outlined in detail. Man is isolated from God. He is lost. He has no hope apart from Christ. Deep within he knows he has sinned and is separated from God. He has good reason to be anxious. Even the Christian feels the loss of fellowship with God when he sins; he too feels anxiety, but for him anxiety may be based more on a faulty belief system of trying to earn God's love.

The medical factors have already been discussed. Treatment recommendations follow. Psychological causes are complex, as is reflected in the treatment approaches (unresolved issues deep within, faulty belief systems, inappropriate learned responses, and too much current stress). The anxiety may be more related to current day stress (A2). It may be more related to repressed hurts of long ago (A1). It may be anxiety over anxiety or whatever obsession, phobia, or mental disorder the individual has (A3). Often there is a combination of all three.

Anxiety does not have to become a danger. Psychological studies confirm that mild anxiety can be helpful. Employees are more productive with mild anxiety, and surgical patients with mild anxiety do better. The Scriptures also indicate that some anxiety (a realistic concern seen in such verses as Phil. 2:20, 2 Cor. 11:28, 1 Cor. 12:25) is healthy. In the early stages, anxiety can also be a signal that something needs to be done. However, intense anxiety (fretting and worrying, as described in such verses as Phil. 4:6, Luke 8:14, and 1 Peter 5:7) is not healthy.

Counseling Approaches to Treat Anxiety

There are many counseling approaches to treating anxiety. In the psychotherapy handbook, over 250 current schools of therapy are listed. It is not our goal to list all of these, but to note some of the common-sense techniques and programs which Christian psychiatry currently uses and which have proven helpful to our patients with anxiety and related disorders. We use a few basic approaches, which are not independent, but interactive in dealing with anxiety.

The Insight-oriented Approach

We have seen many patients who have anxiety because of deep unresolved issues within. Perhaps years ago they were hurt severely at least once, and perhaps repeatedly. As a result, deep hurts and repressed anxieties and emotions developed. These were never dealt with, and later in life, when a similar situation occurs, the anxieties again flair, causing the person to be unable to function. In using the insight approach, we try to encourage the person to share with us these deep secrets and hurts. People have shared for the first time hurts that have bothered them for fifteen or twenty years. As they do so, the tears flow, the emotions come, and they begin, for the first time in their lives, to resolve the hurt. However, these issues are often intense and extensive and not easily or quickly resolved. In part, the counseling process helps this person gain insight into how these deep emotions cause the depression, anxiety, or medical problem today.

Insight also helps them to see how these issues from the past affect their current relationships, such as when anxiety around a certain individual today may be triggered by anxiety about a similar type of personality in the past. Insight also provides an understanding of how we use *defense mechanisms*. We all lie to ourselves in ways that we are not aware of. The anxious individual may very well need to become aware of the different ways he is lying to himself and the ways he is not admitting the truth, the ways he is holding issues inside through these defenses and thus continuing his anxiety. For example, the anxious individual may not be aware that he is projecting his own feelings and shortcomings onto others and reacting to others with anxiety. In Scripture, King Saul used projection to deal with his jealousy and hostility toward David. The anxiety-prone person may need insight into the defense mechanism of isolation, whereby he isolates himself from serious and unacceptable emotions inside of him such as jealousy, greed, or lust. He has split them off from consciousness, affecting his current mood and behavior, yet he has no insight into it. Or he may need insight into rationalization, whereby he has justified unacceptable sinful behavior and attitudes, but lacks insight into what he is doing. These defense mechanisms are listed in more detail in Appendix 2. A key role of insight-oriented counseling is to make individuals aware of issues within and to help them to work through the defense mechanisms they use to hide the truth from themselves.

Insight-oriented counseling can also help a person work through *transference issues*. In counseling, clients often transfer their feelings toward significant people in the past such as their mother or father to the counselor. Furthermore, it is common to transfer feelings of insecurity from individuals we have known in the past to current-day relationships. An individual may have tremendous anxiety around a current relationship, yet be unaware that the current conflict is coming from the past.

A counselor who wants to help an individual gain insight often begins by simply letting the individual talk. The term used in therapy for this venting of emotion is *catharsis*. This often begins with being loving enough to listen to the person share the issues from deep within. It has been said that being listened to and understood is one of the most moving of all experiences.

Such loving support also makes possible what is termed *corrective emotional experience*. An individual sharing issues may transfer feelings from the past to the counselor, whose healthy stability and love should result in a corrective emotional experience.

Insight does not come easily. *Resistance* often develops because it is painful to see issues inside of us that we do not want to look at. To some degree the brain has very carefully arranged these defense mechanisms to protect us. Yet lying to ourselves about issues inside is unhealthy.

Naturally, the amount of insight an individual needs at any point varies. God is very gracious to slowly show us things about ourselves. We suspect that if God showed us how sinful we are all at one time, our egos could scarcely take it. Individuals who are more unstable in their ego structure and closer to being psychotic need a more *supportive approach* without pressing too hard for insight too fast. Individuals who are just having trouble functioning occupationally, socially, or medically are probably capable of more *intense insight*.

Individuals may need *insight into their personalities*. For example, *paranoid* individuals may need to see their use of projection in blaming others. They are preoccupied with justice and fairness. Often, these individuals were raised by harsh parents. Consequently, they have an intense longing to be loved, but have a fear of betrayal. They often have no insight into this fear. They feel rejection, so they reject others. They truly fear closeness. The *obsessive-compulsive personality* may lack insight into obedience-defiance conflicts. Outwardly he submits, but deep within he wants to rebel. He may lack insight into how these conflicts stem from a desire to be overly in control. Or the more *hysterical* person may have little insight into unresolved sexual issues in childhood, perhaps stemming from sexual abuse. Such abuse may have triggered current sexual conflicts, intense surface emotions, or seductive behavior. The *passive-aggressive individual* may have little insight into his half-hearted compliance to try to get even with others, based on past experiences in denying and hiding anger. Other personality types need insights into the defense mechanisms they use in trying to cope with unresolved anger.

THE PAST. Some of the most common past issues that trigger current anxiety include parental absence; loss of one or both parents through divorce, abandonment, rejection issues; parents who are either overly possessive or too harsh; parents being cold or overly symbiotic; or even seductiveness. Issues may revolve around birth order, sibling rivalry, or developing independence. The child may have been given *injunctions* when he was young such as "be perfect" or "not good enough" or "do more" or "don't succeed" or "don't grow up" or even "don't exist." There may also be a lack of insight into other "don't" messages which were given when the child was young, such as "don't be a . . . ," "don't think," "don't feel," "don't be you," "don't do whatever you are doing." Of course an individual should never do anything against the Word of God; however, parents are not perfect and sometimes unhealthy restrictive messages are given. Insight can help the individual determine which injunctions were biblical and healthy and which ones should now be ignored.

These anxious individuals with unresolved past issues will usually behave predictably. Those with unmet dependency needs often become clinging and demanding. They may become angry, on guard, expecting others to disappoint them, testing their love over and over, making greater and greater demands, experiencing rejection, then putting up barriers to avoid closeness with people. These barriers may include having a lot of superficial friends but none very close; adopting the lifestyle of "perpetual victim"; rescuer or persecutor; overeating; abusing alcohol and other harmful substances. Insight into unresolved past issues can help the individual understand—and change—these destructive patterns.

CURRENT ISSUES AND STRESSES. The person may need insight into the fact that he is simply under too much current stress. The Holmes-Rahe Stress Test rates major life changes: For example, death of a spouse = 100 points; divorce = 73 points; marital separation = 65 points; jail term = 63 points; death of family member = 63 points; personal injury or illness = 53 points; marriage = 50 points; fired from work = 47 points; marital reconciliation = 45 points; and retirement = 45 points. Points are even assigned for vacations and Christmas. If the individual receives over 200 points within a year, his likelihood of suffering physical or emotional consequences including anxiety is significant. A person's faulty communication patterns may be caused by anxiety and may intensify the anxiety which is present. The individual may need to learn to listen more and to state feelings using "I feel" messages rather than "you should" assertions. Other current issues may lead to anxiety. For example, a Christian may have drifted away from God, no longer having a daily quiet time or receiving encouragement from the body of Christ, or perhaps even has developed a sinful habit. Most important of all, the individual may never have trusted Christ and thus has a deep anxiety within that can only be resolved with the security of a personal relationship with Christ. This failure to trust Christ could be related to some traumatic event or series of experiences in the past. Perhaps an individual is no longer taking care of himself physically and is overweight, not getting enough sleep, not exercising, and feeling anxious. Holding onto bitterness and carrying grudges can trigger anxiety. Insight into these spiritual, physical, or emotional issues often brings relief from anxiety and leads to worry-free living.

BASIC TECHNIQUES. A counselor uses several techniques to help an individual to work through anxiety patterns. For example, the counselor may want to use *questions* to help a person come to a conclusion that is too anxiety-provoking to reach otherwise. *Reflecting* back to an individual can show the impact of the emotion on others. *Repeating* the last word or the word with the emphasis which seems to be anxiety-related can help the client gain insight.

It is important to know what attitude to use to help an individual gain insight. Most people respond just to a friendly attitude, including those who are anxious or depressed. However, those who are more paranoid may respond better to a *passive friendly attitude*. An individual who has more sociopathic or hysteric traits may respond best to a matter-of-fact, straightforward approach.

Another important factor is *timing*. At times, an individual can receive insight, and other times the defenses are too strong. There are times to be directive and there are times to be more indirect. Nathan in the Bible helped David gain insight by first using the indirect technique. After David had sinned with Bathsheba, the prophet helped him gain insight by telling him the story of a rich man who took the one sheep owned by a poor man. David reacted because of the defense of projection asserting that the rich man should die. At that point Nathan became directive, telling David that he was the man. Another helpful technique is *self-disclosure*. If a therapist shares personal struggles similar to the client's, the client may be more open to admitting his own problems and gaining insight. Another technique, *interpretation*, involves gently explaining some of the individual's attitudes and behaviors, then waiting to see what kind of resistance or acceptance comes in response.

THE GROUP PROCESS. Group therapy has long been used in counseling, but God established the importance of group in New Testament days, as evidenced by the many "one another" passages in the New Testament. Through interacting in the group, an individual may overcome anxiety by learning needed social skills. He may learn to deal with conflicts in the present that symbolize unresolved past conflicts. He may receive advice. He may overcome his fear or anxiety of being with people. He may gain support. He may deal with anxiety vicariously by hearing how someone else overcame a specific conflict similar to his. Certainly, a group emphasis can be important with insight. It is often easier for an individual to accept insight from a group rather than from one individual such as a therapist. Through group therapy one also may learn to overcome anxiety temporarily by assuming the role of someone he has had conflict with, imagine that he is in their shoes and learn how they react and how they feel. Groups also enable an individual to receive feedback on games he might be playing and defenses he might be using. The group solution is almost always superior to individual solutions in attacking the problem.

BIBLICAL PERSPECTIVE ON INSIGHT. An important issue to consider relative to anxiety is the matter of insight. One of the most fundamental principles for Christian counseling is based on Jeremiah 17:9, the premise that "the heart is deceitful above all things and desperately wicked" beyond knowledge. The following verse asserts "I, the LORD, search the hearts." In these two statements, Jeremiah underscores two important principles. First, God knows the thoughts and motives of our hearts. Second, those thoughts and motives are in essence the product of depravity. This is consistent with Jesus' statement in Revelation 2:23, characterizing Himself as "He who searches the minds and hearts." In our ministry we observe a close correlation between man's ability to deceive himself, using the defense mechanisms earlier documented, and the presence and degree of anxiety. We have observed the existence of the conscious mind, in which we are aware, the subconscious mind from which data can be recalled, and an unconscious mind, consisting of things which have been recorded into memory but cannot be recalled into the consciousness or awareness except through traumatic incidents or in therapy.

THE HEART. In Scripture, the heart is viewed as the center of an individual's mental, emotional, and spiritual life, the innermost part, reflecting the real person. There are distinctions of "spirit, soul, and body" (1 Thess. 5:23) and between "soul and spirit" (Hebrews 4:12). The term *heart,* particularly as it is used in the Old Testament, does not look at the organ which pumps blood to the body, but rather at the spiritual person. This can be seen in the use of the term. For example, in 1 Samuel 12:20, Samuel exhorts Israel to "serve the LORD with all your heart." David's warriors were men described in 1 Chronicles 12:33 as "not of double heart" (*The Open Bible,* NAS).

As the center of our thought processes, the heart knows, understands, reflects, considers, and remembers. Solomon is described in 2 Chronicles 1:10 as asking for a wise heart, which God grants (v. 12). Second, the heart is viewed as the emotional center. It is the seat of emotions and desires, of joy and pain, of courage and despair, of fear and anxiety, and of trust. When David expresses his desire to build a temple for God, it is said to be in his heart (1 Kings 8:17–18). Third, the heart is the moral and spiritual center, the point of decision making. This is why it is said that God sees the heart and tests the heart, refines the heart and searches the heart. In 1 Kings 11:4, "when Solomon was old," his many wives and their religious practices "turned away his heart" from God. And his heart was no longer at peace with God, as it had been before. Thus, Solomon, who wrote the Book of Proverbs, which deals so extensively with the heart, failed to follow his own advice.

Scriptures indicate that a person may have an evil heart, be godless in heart, have a perverse or deceitful heart or a hardened heart. It is also possible for a person to have a cleansed heart, or even to receive a new heart (1 Samuel 10:9). Again, it is important to remember that the authors of Scripture were not speaking of a physical organ replacement or transplant, but rather newness of the spiritual person. David, in Acts 13:22, was characterized as a man after God's own heart, a man who would fulfill all God's will. To have a heart for God simply means to obey God. David's warning to his son, Solomon, in 1 Chronicles 28:9 was to serve God "with a loyal heart and with a willing mind." In light of the fact that the Lord searches all hearts and understands every motive and thought, Psalm 94:11 asserts that God "knows the thoughts of man." David asserts this as well in Psalm 139: 2–3: "You understand my thought afar off. You . . . are acquainted with all my ways." In fact, the following verse asserts God's full awareness of our thoughts even before they are expressed in words.

The thoughts of God are held up as far beyond those of man. God's thoughts are intensely deep, just as His works are magnificent, comparing with man's knowledge as brilliance compares to senselessness and stupidity (Psalm 92:5–6). God's thoughts are innumerable, incomprehensible, beyond understanding (Psalm 40:5, 1 Cor. 3:20), yet his thoughts are valuable to us (Psalm 139:17).

Part of the problem is that man's thoughts are depraved. Isaiah 55:7–9 presents a call to the unrighteous to abandon his thoughts and turn in faith to receive God's pardon. God's thoughts and ways are far beyond ours. The "counsels of the wicked" are characterized as "deceitful" in Proverbs 12:5, "arrogant" in Psalm 10:4. At times, wickedness and arrogance infiltrate the lives of believers. For example, Galatians 6:3 says "if anyone thinks himself to be something, when he is nothing, he deceives himself." Second Timothy 3:8 gives two examples of men who opposed God's truth, thus demonstrating their mental depravity (cf. 1 Tim. 6:5). Thus, we as believers have a responsibility to consciously take captive our thought life to the obedience of Christ (2 Cor. 10:5). Often, impure motives (Acts 8:20–22) provide a false, self-deceiving sense of security (1 Cor. 10:12) and lead to not only anxiety, but spiritual failure.

Jesus Christ was able to discern the thoughts and motives of the hearts of individuals during His ministry. This was predicted of Him in Luke 2:35; it can be seen in His ministry to the scribes in Matthew 9:4, and even to His disciples, who had doubts and anxiety in their hearts after His death. In Luke 24:38 when the resurrected Christ appeared in their midst, they were startled and frightened, not understanding their own anxiety and lack of belief. James, the half-brother of the Lord according to the flesh, a leader in the early church, points out how partiality is but one evidence of evil motives (James 2:4). How can we gain insight into our hidden motives? How can we evaluate them to determine whether they are appropriate or sinful? Hebrews 4:12 points out our primary resource is the Word of God. The context of experiencing rest contrasts to anxiety, and in order to avoid disobedience or unbelief, we must utilize the resource of the Word of God. Like a surgeon's scalpel or a two-edged Roman sword, it is sharp; it is also active, and above all it is living, it pierces through to divisions of soul and spirit and body (joints and marrow), and it provides accurate evaluation of our thoughts, conscious and subconscious, and subconscious motives. Verse 13 points out that God sees every heart, that all is open and laid bare before Him.

How should we then respond? Like the psalmist in Psalm 119:59 who says, "I thought about my ways and turned my feet to Your testimonies." The consideration of our emotions and motives should lead to biblical behavior. The psalmist also implores God to search him and know his heart, to evaluate his anxious thoughts, pointing out any hurtful or wicked way and leading him in ways of eternal significance (Ps. 139:23–24). David echoes a similar prayer in light of his perception of God in Psalm 19:14:

> Let the words of my mouth and the meditation of my heart
> Be acceptable in your sight,
> O Lord, my strength and my redeemer.

Significantly, both Psalms 19 and 139 were written by David; both reflect on the greatness and glory of God, who has revealed Himself, but who is also in a personal relationship with the author; both indicate the importance of choosing appropriate thoughts. Psalm 69:5 carries the theme with the assertion "O God, You know my foolishness; / And my sins are not hidden from You." Psalm 32:5 includes David's acknowledgment of his sin. "My iniquity," he says, "I have not hidden. I said 'I will confess my transgressions to the Lord.'" In a related prayer of confession, David in Psalm 51:6 says, "Behold, You desire truth in the inward part, / And in the hidden part You will make me to know wisdom." God places a premium on honesty with ourselves regarding emotions and motives. Furthermore, David points to God's Word as the primary resource to prevent the sinful emotions and motives: "Your word have I hidden in my heart, / That I might not sin against You."

As Solomon warns in Proverbs 4:23, "Keep your heart with all diligence, / For out of it spring the issues of life." To put it another way, as we think within, so we are (Prov. 23:7). Getting in touch with those hidden emotions and motives that produce anxiety, meditating on Scripture, and allowing God's Word to govern our conscious behavior and our thoughts and motives can go a long way to providing worry-free living. Furthermore, when anxiety plagues us, our approach can be that of the psalmist in Psalm 94:19, "In the multitude of my anxieties, / Your comforts delight my soul." The encouragement and insight of God's Word (Rom. 15:4) can aid in resolving anxiety and lead to worry-free living.

Reality Therapy Approach to Anxiety

When deep-seated issues are present, insight-oriented counseling is usually the approach of choice. At other times, a present-day problem-solving approach may be indicated for several reasons. Deep issues may not be present, or a person's ego structure may be so weak that too much insight at one point may cause him to decompensate. At times just common sense would have the counselor be loving and kind, listening, and offering practical advice to overcome anxiety. This advice might include developing a specific plan of action for dealing with current stress. For example, an anxious individual may need to develop a specific plan, perhaps of eight or ten things to do daily or weekly for the next month, to see if this would help overcome the anxiety. This plan might include such things as a daily quiet time, calling a supportive friend once a day, a daily exercise program, a balanced diet, or doing one specific thing this week to resolve a painful issue from the past. This frequently used approach has been best categorized as *Reality Therapy*. The therapist is encouraged to be warm and personal; the client is encouraged to work out a specific behavioral plan to attack the problem and then implement it. Often without being aware of it, individuals have implemented terrible plans for daily living. For example, a depressed person may be sleeping late, not exercising, avoiding social contact, and drinking alcohol or taking drugs, then wonder why the depression gets worse and worse. A present-day problem-solving approach to this scenario would include reversing the negative components of the current "plan," plus memorizing one Scripture verse per day. Feelings and behavior affect each other; but since feelings are more difficult to deal with at times, the behavior should be our initial focus. Specific behavioral changes can lead to a change in feelings.

Guidelines for reality therapy might include:
1. The therapist should *be personal* with the client.
2. Focus on a *specific behavioral plan* of action. A daily and weekly plan, highly specific, should help resolve the problems.
3. The client must make a *commitment to the plan* and is encouraged to follow it totally. If he should decide later to make a new plan, this is fine. But whatever plan he adopts, he should be committed to it for whatever length of time agreed upon, usually a week to a month.
4. *No excuses* are accepted. If necessary, a new plan is made.
5. *Never give up*. Remember, God never gives up on us.

It is often best to combine the two approaches listed above, insight and behavior. In fact, God's plan is to help us see things about ourselves and then gradually to modify behavior and become more Christlike.

Belief System Approach to Anxiety

We all have belief systems that we either adopt intellectually or accept on a feeling level. These affect our present-day lives. Between an event and our behavioral or feeling response is our belief system. In other words, anxiety results not just from an event and the resulting feeling, but from the underlying belief system.

These belief systems may produce intense anxiety and insecurity, and they need to be altered to fit reality. In the medical world, this approach is usually called *Cognitive Therapy;* in the psychological world, this approach is usually called *Rational Emotive Therapy.* In the Christian world Larry Crabb has written extensively about *Cognitive Therapy,* Jay Adams in the area of *Reality Therapy,* and Bruce Narramore about *Insight-oriented* counseling.

ERRONEOUS BELIEFS. The following terms are commonly used in cognitive therapy to describe faulty beliefs: *Personalization*—a mother may feel that a shoe was left in the middle of the floor in an intentional attack on her. *Generalization*—a parent may conclude that a child who misbehaves today will never amount to anything. *Polarization*—issues are seen as black and white, as when a Christian views his pastor and church as either all good or all bad, not recognizing any "gray areas." *Selective Abstraction*—a student focuses on the five points missed during the exam rather than the 95 correct points. *Magnification*—a spouse views as catastrophic or earth-shaking a relatively routine current marital conflict. *Arbitrary inference*—leads an individual to conclude that a group of people on the other side of the room is talking about him. All these faulty beliefs can produce intense anxiety.

FAULTY CHRISTIAN BELIEFS. Some anxiety-producing faulty beliefs are common in Christians, though they may exist more on a feeling level than intellectually. Several of these faulty beliefs follow:
- "God can never forgive me for some past sin," a belief refuted by 1 John 1:9 and Psalm 103:12–14.
- "God cannot use me because I am weak or not completely spiritually strong in all areas," a belief opposed by 2 Corinthians 12:9, "For My strength is made perfect in weakness."
- "God will love me more if I do more for God." God's love cannot be earned; Ephesians 2:8–9 tells us it is simply "by grace . . . through faith . . . the gift of God, not of works."
- "Because I am not prosperous, God's love is no longer with me."
- "I am not important in the body of Christ."
- "I am doomed to a life of loneliness."
- "I must carry my guilt for a certain length of time before I can be forgiven."

It is the counselor's job to redirect these false beliefs to a biblical perspective. He can do this by developing assignments whereby the client can see that his belief systems simply are not true. For example, an individual who believes that he cannot give talks before others may be given the assignment of sharing his testimony with a small group and observing how they respond. The specific evidence helps to overcome his erroneous belief.

When the belief system is faulty, the individual's beliefs cause anxiety. In cognitive therapy, these belief systems are challenged, and then new healthy, anxiety-reducing belief systems are slowly developed.

Behavioral Approaches to Anxiety

Three approaches or models for counseling have been described for use in overcoming anxiety: the insight-oriented approach, the belief-system approach, and the present-day problem solving approach. The behavior approach is often considered under the third of these. We list it separately because it provides an extensive number of techniques for use with anxiety.

Behavior therapists believe that anxiety can be a learned response. Furthermore, they believe that anxiety can become a conditioned response to a neutral stimulus when it is paired with an anxiety-provoking stimulus. Thus, if anxiety can be learned, it can be unlearned. Many techniques have been developed for this process.

We know that all the premises behind behavior therapy are not valid. Our major concern regarding the behavioral school is that it often focuses on symptoms rather than underlying issues. Anxiety is multifactorial, including current stress, unresolved past issues, perhaps a medical or genetic component, and possibly learned behavior as well. To focus on any one aspect and ignore the others would be naive. Yet we do feel that we can learn from this school just as we can learn from others. Although the behavior approach seems to work more at a symptom level, the individual with intense anxiety can benefit even from symptomatic relief. Some of the techniques follow:

RELAXATION TECHNIQUES. Here the individual is taught *how* to relax. Anxiety produces significant muscle tension, which in turn intensifies the anxiety response. In other words, anxiety becomes a signal to become more anxious. We often use relaxation to teach the individual that anxiety is a signal to relax and turn to Scripture meditation. The individual is taught to breathe deeply, exhale, and relax the muscles. In using the technique the individual is told to tighten various muscle groups, then use that tightness as a signal to relax, just as he should when anxiety is coming upon him at any time. The client may be told to clench his fist and experience all the anxiety in his fist, then to relax his hands and to remember that anxiety is a signal to relax. At the same time he is told to breathe in and then, as he exhales, to relax. He works through different muscles of his body until his entire body is relaxed and until he has begun to learn the conditioned response that anxiety is a signal to relax.

TIME LIMIT TO WORRIES. Some individuals, especially the obsessive-compulsives, worry all the time. They can be encouraged to set a fifteen-minute time limit on worries, either once or twice a day. Often, the brain will release worry if it realizes it has a designated period in which to focus in on that issue. Rather than focus on the issues twenty-four hours a day, a time limit is placed on the worries. This frees a lot of mental energy. When the worried thoughts intrude during the day, individuals are encouraged simply to jot down what the thoughts are and to remind themselves that they will have a time that day to focus on those worries and possible solutions. Often, over time the individual even forgets to "worry" at the designated time!

THOUGHT-STOPPING TECHNIQUE. The brain tends to respond to what it is commanded to do, and this does seem to help some individuals. One is encouraged to silently say when worrying begins, "Stop." We have had limited success with this technique, but other research reports better results.

DESENSITIZATION. This technique conditions or desensitizes one to the situation about which he is fearful or anxious. For example, a person who fears flying may be told initially to sit in a chair and think about his next plane trip. The counselor slowly leads him from beginning to prepare for the flight to thinking through the whole flight experience. Each time he becomes anxious, the counselor encourages the individual to breathe in, then relax. Anxiety, again, becomes a signal to relax. After all this is worked through mentally, then it is worked through physically. There may be homework: the individual is assigned to drive back and forth to the airport until he can do this without growing anxious. Next, he may be assigned to go into the terminal. Thus, the individual is slowly desensitized to the anxiety-producing situation. Great success has been achieved with those who fear flying, elevators, crowds, and so on.

POSITIVE REINFORCEMENT. Desired behavior is simply reinforced, for example through verbal compliments. A person may be rewarded and encouraged for not being so anxious or for appearing more calm and relaxed. This reinforces the desired behavior and helps to alleviate the undesired anxiety.

EXTINCTION. Extinction is a behavior technique whereby undesired behavior is not reinforced. For example, some individuals receive reinforcement for anxiety and gain a lot of attention from being anxious. With this technique, the counselor and family members give less reinforcement and less attention to the individual when he is anxious and more attention when he is relaxed and at ease.

AVERSIVE CONDITIONING. Aversive conditioning is a technique in which an individual receives negative or unpleasant response when he is anxious. Through such conditioning, the individual begins to associate anxiety with pain; therefore, the anxiety begins to go away. Aversive conditioning techniques have often been used to treat smokers. In some cases, when a person is anxious and turns to smoking, he is popped with a rubber band worn at the wrist whenever he lights up. The aversive experience can slowly lead to loss of the desire to smoke.

COMPETING BEHAVIOR. When a person feels anxious, he is instructed to begin some kind of competing behavior. For example, he may be told to take out a note pad and write down what he is doing as the anxiety begins. This can provide both insight into the trigger for anxiety and a competing behavior which may lessen the anxiety.

CONTINGENCY CONTRACTING. The person receives some kind of tangible, meaningful reward when he is not anxious. The belief is that thereby anxiety would slowly be avoided.

MODELING. In modeling, an anxious individual is instructed to spend time with individuals who are easygoing, relaxed, and not anxious.

PARADOXICAL INTENTION. If one is anxious, then he is instructed to try to become more anxious with this technique. The belief is that the person becomes so annoyed with the massed practice of being anxious that the anxiety actually decreases. We seldom use this technique in the Christian world because it may violate our belief system. Yet this technique can be used with sudden anxiety-related problems as insomnia. The client is instructed to try to stay awake, and the result is often sleep.

FLOODING. It is believed that if one is flooded with the anxiety-provoking situation, the anxiety may actually decrease. For example, a person who has a fear of heights may be taken to the top of a skyscraper and instructed to walk near the edge. The basic strategy is to prevent the client from escaping the fearsome situation, concentrating on it for a time until the anxiety begins to break down. This technique is seldom used by Christian counselors but is common with some secular therapists.

ASSERTIVENESS TRAINING. Timid individuals often turn their feelings inward and become anxious. If they learn to become more assertive, to ask for what they need or want and express how they feel in an adult manner, anxiety may decrease.

SYMPTOM REPORTING. The individual is instructed to write down all of the symptoms every time he has anxiety. The belief is that his response to this practice will slowly decrease the anxiety.

REPETITION OF MOTOR HABIT. There may be some habit associated with anxiety, such as rubbing the hands together. The individual is instructed to repeat the action until the desire to do it—and the associated anxiety—decreases.

Some of these techniques may seem superficial at best and some even humorous. However, many individuals have received symptom relief by using them. We have found most helpful instruction in breathing and relaxation, instruction in limiting worries to a specific time, and desensitization, usually with insight. Balanced assertiveness and positive reinforcement have also proven effective.

Medical Approaches for Anxiety

First, the counselor needs to be aware of the dangers of not dealing with ongoing anxiety (psychophysiologic disorders).

Second, any medical disease that may produce anxietylike symptoms should be treated (mitral valve prolapse, temporal lobe epilepsy, pheochomocytoma, hyperthyroidism, and so on).

Third, medication for anxiety should be used but only with judgment and great care. Several types of medicines are available. An evaluation of each type follows:

Minor tranquilizers (Valium, Librium, Ativan, Centrax, Klonopin, Paxipam, Serax, Xanax, Miltown, Tranxene, etc.) have been the mainstay of treatment. Minor tranquilizers work in association with the neurotransmitter GABA, which is directly associated with the anxiety response. Valium has sold more than any drug in history. These tranquilizers definitely relieve anxiety. Their major shortcoming has been their addiction potential. Our belief is that they can be used if: 1) underlying issues are also dealt with; 2) they are used short term so that they do not become addicting and tolerance does not develop; 3) the anxiety is severe, disabling, and not just a signal of danger. Sleeping pills (Dalmane, Halcion, Restoril, etc.) also fit this category and are also addicting if used long term (around thirty days). Nonaddicting tranquilizers are being developed. Buspar is the first to be released. Overall, it seems less effective.

Antihistamines (especially Vistaril) have also been used for anxiety relief. Vistaril is nonaddictive, but is usually much less effective.

Major tranquilizers have also been used for anxiety relief. Since these medicines are actually antipsychotics (or neuroloptics) that alter the neurotransmitter dopamine and thereby alter cognition and correct perceptions, this title is really a misnomer. The major tranquilizers do relieve anxiety, but this is certainly not their major action. Also, these are potent drugs with potentially dangerous side effects and should not be used for routine anxiety. They should be used only in cases of psychosis.

Beta blockers are also used for anxiety. They block the peripheral effects of anxiety such as rapid heart beat and tremor. They block the peripheral effects of catodrolamins in the autonomic nervous system. They have classically been used as antihypertensive medicine and in certain forms of heart disease. Indurol, Tenormin, Corgand are just a few of many.

Antidepressants have also been used in anxiety disorders—especially panic disorders, which are believed to have a somewhat different biochemical and neurologic pathway than other anxiety disorders. Tofranil, Elavil, Sinequan, Surmontil, Pamalor, Ascendin, and Prozac are a few. These drugs are not addicting but generally are not very effective for anxiety. One exception is in panic episodes. These drugs act primarily on the neurotransmitters serotonin and norepinephrine.

Atypical antidepressants (Monamine oxidase (MAO) inhibitors) are often used in depressive disorders that have anxiety as a major component. Nardil and Parnate are two such drugs.

Finally, other medical approaches have been used in history. Electric shock therapy (EST) is used more for severe depression than anxiety. Although lobotomy has been used for intractable anxiety, we do not recommend this. Insulin coma, once used for various mental disorders including severe anxiety, is no longer used.

Common Sense Approaches

Many common sense approaches can aid in overcoming anxiety. Some have been described already in the main text of this book.

Exercise

Exercise probably helps to relieve anxiety in several ways. First, it provides a diversion for worries. Second, exercise releases not only adrenalin but also endorphins and enkephalins that may very well lift moods. It is very possible that the jogger's high is not all psychological, but may be medical as well. As William Glasser predicted in his book *Positive Addiction,* an individual may actually become addicted to exercise in both psychological and physical ways. Finally, exercise helps in the sense that the better the individual's physical condition, the more he is prepared to withstand anxiety.

Sleep

When entering the hospital many of our patients are extremely anxious. After a night or two of sleep, they seem much improved. When an individual gets fewer than four or five hours sleep per night for any significant period of time, his chance of dying is increased. During World War II the enemy designed experiments to produce extreme anxiety and mental decompensation in our troops that had been captured. The enemy would simply awaken an individual every time he went to sleep. He would become irritable, confused, and anxious and even answer questions to which he should not have responded. At one time a type of therapy known as sleep therapy was actually developed for mental disorders. Although this is not used a great deal today, it is safe to say that sleep helps relieve anxiety.

Music

In some research studies, when individuals were asked the most moving experience of their lives, many listed something related to music. One can learn to use music to relax and overcome anxiety. Of course, the type of music is important. We recommend the old hymns of the faith. Many have words that address anxiety specifically. Also, the very nature of the music is relaxing. The titles of some of the old hymns illustrate how they can replace anxiety—"Never Alone," "Tell It to Jesus," "What a Friend We Have in Jesus," "The Lily of the Valley," "Sweet Hour of Prayer," "Love Lifted Me," " 'Tis So Sweet to Trust in Jesus." Even the paranoid King Saul relaxed when David played the harp.

Talking to a Friend

Through the ages, this has been one of the major commonsense approaches to overcoming anxiety. Yet in our culture many people do not even have one person they feel is an intimate friend, with whom they can share their deepest anxieties and still feel accepted. We all need a half dozen to a dozen close friends with whom we can share any anxiety and concern and yet feel accepted. The authors make it a personal habit to share with a close friend any bothersome issue of the day. Sharing with a friend helps in several ways; it simply helps to dispel anxiety surrounding current issues. It keeps us from turning the anxiety inward, and furthermore it helps a person be more objective about any issue or anxiety he is wrestling with.

Action Plan

The details of this are listed under Reality Therapy Approach (p. 186). For example, a student who is anxious over an upcoming exam would devise a study plan, then sit down and study for the test.

The Worst-case Approach

In considering the anxiety, one should think of the worst that could happen, then evaluate why that would not be so bad after all. For example, a financially strapped individual might list his worst case as bankruptcy. Yet if he should go bankrupt, his working day and night would be over and there would be benefit and resolution even in that bad situation. As Romans 8:28 points out, "All things work together for good to those who love God."

Recreation and Laughter

It has been said that laughter relieves more tension than crying and is certainly a lot more fun. It is likely that endorphins and enkephalins are released with laughter, which help to overcome anxiety.

List Your Five Big Worries

Ninety-five percent of all the things we worry about never come true. It is helpful sometimes to sit down and list your five big worries five years ago to see how many of them came true. Usually, they did not.

Take Vacations

Get away from your usual routine. Many anxious and obsessive-compulsive individuals take vacations that center around work. If they can gradually begin to learn to take vacations that are more oriented toward relaxation and just fun, then anxiety can be decreased.

A Regular Medical Checkup

Have a medical checkup once a year. Personal health is one of the biggest sources of worry. Much of this anxiety can be relieved by having a good medical checkup once a year or a more in-depth examination if indicated.

Don't Put Things Off

Do an adequate job, and consider the job done. Many anxious and obsessive individuals are so perfectionistic they keep putting off jobs in order to do a perfect job later. When they delay, they become more and more anxious. It is better to do an adequate job and to do it at the time rather than to put it off and keep worrying about it. Also, many perfectionists are filled with guilt if they do not accomplish a long list of duties every day. We encourage listing a reasonable number of things each day, trying to get them done, then accepting and acknowledging the good about what they have done.

Spiritual Approaches

Most of these have been explained in the text of the book, but because of their importance, they will be summarized here. A biblical and theological summary of anxiety and fear will follow. The spiritual approaches are not to be taken independently of other approaches; all are interrelated.

Four Categories of Spiritual Problems

In our practice we have observed spiritual problems in four broad categories, all of which are related to anxiety.

1. Every person, including the anxious individual, *needs to know Christ* as his personal Savior. He needs to hear and act on such verses as Romans 3:23, Romans 6:23, and John 1:12, which explain that Christ was the Son of God, that He died on the cross for our sins, and that each of us needs to place trust in the Savior. Many individuals spend much of a lifetime working to overcome insecurities and anxieties, only to realize that the most basic answer is free—the grace of God found through trusting Christ as Savior.

2. Anxious Christians may be *immature* in the Christian life. In fact, none of us is completely mature. The individual may lack balance in some of the basics of Christian living such as time in the Word, prayer, fellowship with Christian believers, and witnessing. Such imbalance may lead to overemphasis in one of

these areas while ignoring others. Growth in Christ is evidenced by the presence of the fruit of the Spirit, including "love, joy, peace . . ." (Gal. 5:22). A lack of peace—anxiety—may evidence a lack of maturity.

3. Some anxious individuals may be committing *a specific sin.* Three broad areas of sin are described in 1 John 2:16–17; *"lust of the flesh,"* such as sexual immorality, overuse of food, alcohol or drugs; *"lust of the eyes,"* materialistic focus; or the *"pride of life,"* which could involve bitterness, arrogance, and control issues. Proverbs 8:36 asserts that the one who sins against God injures himself. Yet, the specific area of sin is sometimes not easily recognized, unless it involves acting out. Other defense mechanisms, such as denial, projection, intellectualization, rationalization, and so on, described previously, are also sinful, but harder to spot. Anxious teenagers often deal with their anxiety by acting out sinful behavior, which only leads to more anxiety.

4. A less common category of spiritual problem is *demonic influence.* There are about sixty-five references to demons in the New Testament. Since they existed in the New Testament days, demons undoubtedly exist today. There is a danger of going to extremes, "seeing demons behind every bush" and using them to avoid personal responsibility. Sometimes anxious individuals blame everything on the devil, refusing to take responsibility for personal choices. Demon possession may be difficult to diagnose, but demonic influence is much more common, affecting every Christian. Satan may use his awareness of our weaknesses, including the tendency to be anxious, to render the Christian ineffective for Christ. Ephesians 6:12 points out that "we do not wrestle against flesh and blood, but against principalities, against powers, against spiritual hosts of wickedness in the heavenly places." First Peter 5:8 described Satan as "a roaring lion, seeking whom he may devour."

Counseling Verbs from Scripture

The approach to treat anxiety in general must be comprehensive since there is no single approach, physical, psychological, or spiritual. In similar fashion there is no single spiritual approach to overcoming problems—anxiety included.

For example, in 1 Thessalonians 5:14, the apostle Paul uses five verbs to describe techniques for relating to, helping, or counseling individuals. Each of these has implications for the Christian counselor today. The first verb, *exhort,* and the last, *be patient,* can apply to all people; in fact, *exhort* is used as an imperative in this fashion in verse 11. Everyone needs counsel and exhortation, and every person being counseled will test the counselor's patience. The three verbs in the middle of the verse reminded the Thessalonians of ways to relate to people with specific problems. For example, those who were unruly needed to be warned or *confronted.* Those who were faint-hearted and at the point of giving up needed to be comforted or *cheered up.* Those who were chronically weak needed to be *supported* or strengthened.

The implication for treating anxiety is obvious. Some anxiety is caused by overt sin. The appropriate approach is confrontation. Some anxiety may be due to a crisis in a life situation. Encouragement and cheer are the proper approaches. Other people may be anxious due to a weakness, perhaps in their belief system. They may need longer term support.

In encouraging those who are anxious, we have found it helpful to communicate several spiritual principles.

1. *Realize that God is with you.* Throughout Scripture the presence of God is seen as a powerful antidote to fear and anxiety. Over 350 times Scripture reminds us, "Fear not." Many of these, such as Isaiah 41:10, directly link this prohibition to God's presence. Moses endured adversity because of his awareness of God's presence (Heb. 11:27). Joshua was reminded of God's presence as he faced the incredible task of assuming leadership over Israel (Josh. 1:5). With the large divorce rate and increasing number of orphans and single-parent children, the promise of Psalm 27:10 provides encouragement against anxiety: "When my father and my mother forsake me, then the LORD will take care of me."

2. *Use prayer.* A. W. Tozier once wrote, "Men are constantly looking for better methods. God is looking for better men—men of prayer." Luke 18:1, among many other passages of Scripture, warns us to pray rather than give up in times of adversity. In 1 Chronicles 4:10 Jabez faced the future by praying that God would "enlarge his territory" and be with him—and God granted him what he requested. James 5:17 reminds us of the effectiveness of prayer in changing circumstances, not only in withholding rain in Elijah's day, but in our lives today as well.

3. *Tap into the resources of the body of Christ.* John Donne once wrote, "No man is an island entire of itself." The evidence of Scripture is that God never intended for any man or woman in the body of Christ to be an island, a "lone ranger." Galatians 6:2 exhorts us to "bear one another's burdens, and so fulfill the law of Christ." Although Paul underscores personal responsibility later in the passage, "each one shall bear his own load" (v. 5), whenever one is "over-burdened," as everyone is at times, the body of Christ can help. The Book of Proverbs is filled with exhortations about the nature and benefits of friendship. Friends are loving (17:17), loyal (18:24, 27:10), refreshing (27:9), willing to be honest (27:6), and mutually beneficial (27:17). Most believers consider the apostle Paul the epitome of a godly Christian. Yet even Paul could openly verbalize his feelings and be vulnerable (2 Tim. 4:9–21). An anxious Christian worker who felt his work had been in vain was significantly encouraged by Hebrews 6:10, "For God is not unjust to forget your work and labor of love which you have shown toward His name, in that you have ministered to the saints, and do minister." Giving and receiving help and encouragement can alleviate anxiety.

4. *Practice positive thinking.* More will be said of this in the theological section, but in Philippians 4:8–9 in the context of replacing anxiety with prayer (v. 6), we're told to focus our thoughts on positive things. Many anxious individuals have discovered great help from practicing Psalm 103:1–2, "Bless the LORD. . . . And forget not all His benefits." Often keeping a daily "benefits list" helps.

5. *Live one day at a time.* Another key passage on anxiety, also to be considered later, is Jesus' discussion in Matthew 6. The Savior's concluding remarks (v. 34) reminded his hearers that there will be enough worry for tomorrow. "Sufficient for the day is its own trouble." Since God cares for sparrows, wildflowers, and other less significant parts of creation, we know He cares for us and is in charge of the future. Thus we are encouraged to replace anxiety with living one day at a time.

6. *Obey God.* Over and over Scripture commands us, "Stop being anxious." Christ (Matt. 6:34), Paul (Phil. 4:6), and Peter (1 Pet. 5:7) all repeat this instruction. Furthermore, Scripture is filled with the command, "Fear not." Our willingness to obey God can motivate us to use the techniques described in this book to give up anxiety and experience worry-free living.

7. *Use God's Word.* The longest chapter in Scripture is Psalm 119. It is devoted to extolling the value of Scripture. In fact, in verse 24 David describes the verses of Scripture as our "counselors." Jeremiah expresses the joy to be experienced by feeding on God's Word (Jer. 15:16). Jesus describes God's Word as eternal (Matt. 24:35). John refers to it as a source of strength (1 John 2:14). Hebrews 4:12 points to the Word as the tool by which we understand our hidden emotions and motives. Thus the Word is perhaps our most important resource for overcoming anxiety.

Suggested Memory Verses Dealing with Anxiety-related Issues

1. ASSURANCE OF SALVATION
    John 10:27–30; John 6:35–37; 1 John 5:11–13; John 3:16–18; John 1:12
2. ASSURANCE OF GOD'S FORGIVENESS
    1 John 1:9; Psalm 103:12–14
3. ASSURANCE OF ANSWERED PRAYER
    1 John 5:14; John 16:24; John 14:13–14; Jeremiah 33:3; Matthew 7:7–8
4. MARRIAGE CONFLICTS
    Ephesians 5:22–23; Colossians 3:18–19; 1 Peter 3:1–7; 1 Corinthians 7:1–5
5. PARENT-CHILD CONFLICTS
    Deut. 6:4–9; Ephesians 6:1–4; Colossians 3:20–21; Proverbs 13:24; Proverbs 29:15
6. LONELINESS
    Hebrews 13:5; Matthew 28:19; Exodus 33:7; Psalm 139:1–6
7. ANGER
    Ephesians 4:26–27; Leviticus 19:17–18; Romans 12:15–16; Proverbs 15:1; Proverbs 19:11; Ecclesiastes 7:9; Colossians 3:8; Matthew 5:21–24
8. BITTERNESS
    Hebrews 13:12; Ephesians 4:31; Acts 8:23; Proverbs 14:10
9. FORGIVING OTHERS
    Ephesians 4:31; 2 Corinthians 2:7; Luke 6:37; Matthew 6:14; Mark 11:25
10. OVERCOMING DEPRESSION
    Psalm 42:5, 11; Psalm 43:5; Genesis 4:6–7; John 14:1
11. TRIALS
    James 1:2–5; 1 Peter 1:6–7; Job 23:10; Romans 5:1–5; Philippians 1:27; 1 Peter 4:12–19
12. SUFFERING
    2 Corinthians 4:7–18; 1:3–4; 12:7–10; Hebrews 12:5–11; Romans 8:28–29; Romans 5:15; John 9:1–3; Mark 5:21–42; 1 Peter 1:3–9

13. TEMPTATION

> 1 Corinthians 10:12-13; Hebrews 4:15-16; Proverbs 4:12; James 4:7-8; Proverbs 8:32

14. ANXIETY

> John 14:27; Philippians 4:6-8; Matthew 6:25-34; Psalm 27:1; 27:14; 34:4; 56:3

Dynamic Scriptural Therapy

The three-pound human brain is one of the most incredible objects in God's creation. It would probably take a computer the size of the Pentagon just to carry out the basic thought processes of the brain, without even considering creativity. The brain contains over 100 billion nerve cells, each individual cell connected with 10,000 other neurons. Memory is stored in this vast array of neurons: *conscious* memory, when we are aware of something happening; *subconscious,* when we are not immediately aware of an event or bit of knowledge but can recall it to awareness; and the *unconscious,* which we may not become aware of except for trauma situations or perhaps in therapy.

Given the existence of the unconscious mind, it is imperative that we somehow integrate Scripture into the mind in order to use it in our lives. Thus we have developed a technique called *Dynamic Scriptural Therapy,* which consists of two components: memorizing and meditating on Scripture. One of the most important techniques we use in dealing with anxiety is to "get people into God's Word and get God's Word into people." Several practical suggestions can be offered for the first step, memorization.

1. *Do it.* Many people never memorize Scripture simply because they are afraid to start. You can start with easy verses or verses you enjoy. Avoid becoming overloaded.

2. *Use practical techniques.* We have found helpful using memory cards as well as continued repetition. We often circle, mark, or date verses in our Bibles and even keep Scripture verses on our desks or tables at home.

3. *Establish a system of accountability.* The authors frequently share memorized verses with each other and will often challenge each other and other friends regarding memorization.

4. *Never give up.* It may not be as easy as when we were younger, but it certainly can be beneficial.

The second important principle is meditation. This is described in Dr. Meier's book *Meditating for Success.* A major issue in meditation is to get the Scripture from our minds and into our hearts and lives. We have earlier described the heart as the unconscious seat of intellect, emotions, and will. As we think about Scripture, mulling it over in our minds, musing upon it, and considering how it affects our lives, we find that Scripture ultimately changes our behavior. Perhaps the best summary of dynamic scriptural therapy is found in Psalm 77: "I will remember" (v. 11)—memorization; "I will also meditate" (v. 12)—meditation. Memorizing and meditating on Scripture can have a dynamic impact in helping an individual overcome anxiety.

APPENDIX 5

ANXIETY—A BIBLICAL AND THEOLOGICAL PERSPECTIVE

WORRY-FREE LIVING HAS been written to provide the reader with resources to understand and cope with anxiety. Because of the authors' strong conviction that biblical truth must undergird our approach to every problem, this biblical and theological section is included. Christians often tend to be a bit more perfectionistic than non-Christians. Many Christians are conscientious and have a desire to walk with the Lord, so they may worry a little more. Furthermore, because they have a fallen nature, they may have a tendency not to want to look at the truth about hidden emotions or motives that are inconsistent with Scripture. The resulting internal conflict produces anxiety.

In the Psalms, anxiety can be seen to arise as a result of guilt over sin (Ps. 51) or the threat of troubles or an enemy (Ps. 102:7; Ps. 69:1–2). The antidote is God's protective care (Ps. 27:5), experienced when we "cast our burden upon Him" (Ps. 55:22).

The Term *Anxiety*

Old Testament

In the Old Testament, one important word for anxiety is *kera,* an Aramaic term, which describes a state of distress. Daniel uses it to describe his distressed spirit (Dan. 7:15). A second Old Testament term is *charadah,* which is used positively of the protective care of the Shunammite woman for Elisha (2 Kings 4:13). A third term, *darash,* is used of God's watchful and attentive care over the promised land and its Israelite inhabitants (Deut. 11:12).

Another Old Testament word for which *merimna* is used in the Septuagint is *daag,* which means "to be afraid, careful." The derivative, *daga,* means care, anxiety. The root, *daag,* is often used of anxiety. Sometimes it can carry the meaning of fear. For example, Saul left off searching for his father's asses because he feared that his father would feel anxiety, because of the time spent in the search (1 Samuel 9:5; 10:2).

Isaiah asks the harlot, Israel, who it was that brought such fear and worry on her that she turned to idolatry without thinking of the Lord (Isaiah 57:11).

Jeremiah portrays the attitude of a man who trusts in God in the midst of invasion as untroubled (nonanxious) by such events (17:8, paraphrasing Psalm 1); he draws strength from his relationship with God.

Zedekiah refuses to surrender to the Babylonians (Jer. 38:19) because he is

199

concerned or anxious about the Jews who have gone over to the Babylonians. In fact, he feared that they would harm him.

The noun form, *daga,* means care, carefulness, fear, sorrow, heaviness. The tribes which settled east of the Jordan expressed a proper anxiety that their children would forget God. Therefore, they set up an altar, not for sacrifice, but rather to remind future generations of their duty to serve the Lord together with the tribes living west of the Jordan (Josh. 22:24). It is also used of heaviness of heart (Prov. 12:25).

Another of the Old Testament Hebrew terms, *ragaz,* has the primary meaning of "to quiver." It is the word used of any emotion, especially anger or fear, which has a physical component. This broad term can mean "to be afraid, to stand at awe, to be enraged, to tremble, to be troubled, to be upset, to be fretful." The word is so used in 1 Chronicles 17:9 in God's Word to David regarding the future for Israel: "They may dwell in a place of their own and move no more." In this passage the idea of being distracted is contrasted with dwelling securely in the place which God willed for them as a people. It is so used of horses and donkeys that were tied so that they could not be moved (2 Kings 7:10). Its key significance in terms of us is to describe an anxiety- or fear-free or stable condition, but without being moved or stirred. Perhaps the most important such verse in the Old Testament is Psalm 55:22:

> Cast your burden on the LORD,
> And He shall sustain you;
> He shall never permit the righteous *to be moved.*

The significance of this truth is that anxiety, the negative, distracting kind that leaves our lives shaken, does not originate from God. Furthermore, when we "cast our burden upon Him" (cf. Ps. 37:4–5), His sustaining power will allow us to overcome the distraction of anxiety. This same concept is seen throughout Psalm 37, particularly in verse 19—"They will not be shaken (distracted). In time of evil and in days of famine, they will have abundance." In fact, Psalm 37 presents several practical keys for overcoming anxiety in its series of imperatives at the beginning of the Psalm—"do not fret because of evildoers," "trust in the LORD," "do good," "dwell in the land," "feed on his faithfulness," "delight yourself . . . in the LORD," "commit your way to the LORD," "trust . . . in Him," "rest in the LORD," "wait patiently for Him," "Do not fret over the prosperity of the wicked," "Cease from anger and wrath," and finally, "wait on the LORD / And keep His way." In essence, Psalm 37 is a practical prescription from the psalmist based on his walk in close personal fellowship with God. We're to deal with the anxious cares of life as he did.

New Testament

The major term for anxiety *merimna,* the noun, comes from the idea of a distraction or a care. It originates from the verb, *merizo,* which means "to part, to share or apportion." From this idea developed the concept of distributing or dividing; thus, *merimnao* means "to be anxious about" or "to be distracted." The term *merimnao* has a wide range of meaning just like the English phrase *to care.* It can be positive in the sense of careful or negative in the sense of overly anxious, distracted, or even distraught. Philosophers were said in the Greek language of the New Testament era to have "brooding" or caring emotions.

In extrabiblical first-century literature, *merizo* is used in the sense of "to distribute" or "to assign." Some uses describe assigning land to a member of the family or the distribution or paying out of money from the public treasury. The term is also used in the basic sense of anxiety. For example, one Greek document reads, "if the next toe quiver, he will be involved in much anxiety and distress; pray to Zeus." Even the pagan Greeks both recognized physical symptoms and saw prayer as an antidote to anxiety. In fact, this term was the basis for Shakespeare's "*uneasy* lies the head that wears a crown." Similar Greek inscriptions regarding "care and watchfulness" give the positive idea of anxiety or distraction: "If you pay attention, you would preserve the kingdom." At times, the verb simply means "to be occupied with," as, for example, when Oedipus asks the herdsmen, "What are you occupied with as a way of life?" In one rather interesting piece of extra-biblical literature, a man named Titedios was renamed Amaremnaus when he became a Christian, apparently to mark him as a man who "chose to take no thought" or not to be anxious, consistent with the injunction of Matthew 6:34.

In the New Testament, the basic idea of *merimna* is to be drawn in different directions or distracted; thus, that which distracts often causes a care, especially an anxious care. When we are anxious, we become distracted from fulfilling that which is best for us, and we cannot enjoy peaceful, worry-free living. The negative adjective *amerimnas* is to be free from care, for example, in Matthew 28:14. The verb *merimnao* means "to take thought, to be anxious about, to have a distracting care, to be careful for." Of the twenty-five uses of terms related to *merizo* in the New Testament, five of them are positive, denoting taking appropriate care. The rest indicate a distraction or anxiety which is less than healthy.

Anxiety As the Lord Spoke of It

Perhaps the major New Testament discussion of *anxiety* is the extended statement from Jesus Christ in what is commonly called the Sermon on the Mount (Matthew 6). This statement also represents the individual uses of the term. Jesus' listeners included many devout religious individuals, a number of whom were looking for and anticipating the coming of the Messiah promised in the Old Testament. Yet their hearts and minds were not ready. In this extended discourse, Christ carefully explains to them the need for a change of mind (repentance) that would lead to a change of life. In this message He presents His personal offer of the kingdom to Israel; yet His statements contain significant principles related to fast-paced life today. In essence His statements relative to anxiety can be summarized under the idea that proper priorities can help eliminate the problem of anxiety.

The first focus in this section is on the *problem* of anxieties. Six times in ten verses the Lord uses the term for *merizo* or *merimna*, three times He gives a negative command, once relative to the present (v. 25) and twice relative to the future. The force of these instructions is literally to say "stop being anxious." The several key causes of anxiety are cited by our Lord in these passages: for example, making a living, providing basic essentials such as food and clothing (v. 25), obtaining possessions to keep up with "the Gentiles" in the rat race of life (vv. 31–32), and concerns about the future and what will happen tomorrow or next year (v. 34).

Thus, our Lord presents anxiety as a real problem, yet one which is really not necessary. In His discussion Jesus uses several illustrations from life to indicate that anxiety is unnecessary. He points out that birds do not worry about grocery money or gardening (v. 26) and that wildflowers do not get uptight over fashion (v. 28). Furthermore, worry will not help us deal with physical deficiencies (v. 27). Three other references to anxiety are also found (vv. 27, 28, 34).

The hidden agenda in anxiety is often perfectionism or a lack of faith. This is seen clearly in the phrase "Oh ye of little faith" (v. 30). In essence, one basic hidden emotion or motive is that we do not trust God to run the universe, to care for our needs, or to work things out the way we desire. This Jesus describes as a lack or deficiency of faith. Thus, anxiety is unbelief in disguise. At one point, one of the authors was working on this portion of the book while riding a plane across a storm front between Dallas and Indianapolis. Who was in control at the time? Was the author, who was sitting in the plane dictating? Was the pilot, whose hands were on the controls? Or was the God who controls the weather and principles of aerodynamics and who provides personal care and concern for His children, including the author? The answer is obvious. God is in control. The more we recognize and live in light of this knowledge, the less we are plagued by anxiety. Thus, a major spiritual antidote for anxiety involves developing personal trust in the God who not only controls the universe, but also cares about the little things, "even the hairs of our head." That we can trust Him and should develop trust in Him is also present in the parallel passage, Mark 13:11.

Closely related to this command to trust is the imperative found in the familiar Matthew 6:33, "But seek first the kingdom of God and His righteousness, and all these things shall be added to you." This underscores the importance of the principle of proper priorities. In essence, the way we develop trust is to obey. The concept "to" seek is vividly illustrated in the experience from the early life of Christ, who was taken at the age of twelve by his mother and stepfather to the temple to celebrate one of the Jewish feasts (Luke 2:41–50). When they discovered Jesus missing on their return trip to Nazareth, Mary and Joseph returned to Jerusalem and *sought* him. Any parent who has had a child turn up missing knows this was not a casual investigation, but a matter of utmost priority. To denote the priority we are to give His authority (kingdom) and His standards (righteousness), Jesus uses the same term used by His mother, Mary, who sought for Him when He was twelve. This principle of priorities can be seen as an elaboration of Jesus' statement in Matthew 6:24, "No one can serve two masters." Though it may seem simplistic, the essence of Jesus' promise is that if we make following Him a life priority, we will eliminate many of the causes for anxiety, thus nipping the problem in the bud.

On several other occasions, the Savior addresses the issue, though not in at such length. For example, in Matthew 10:19, Jesus warns His followers against anxiety about how to respond in the face of persecution from hostile sources, pointing out that God's Spirit will direct their response. In His "sermon by the seashore," another significant milestone in His ministry, Jesus points out, while interpreting the parable of the sower, how the individual "received seed among thorns . . . hears the word, and the *cares* of this world and the deceitfulness of riches choke the word, and he becomes unfruitful" (Matt. 13:22). What an accurate description of how anxiety often functions today. The age in which we are living is significantly marked by affluence. Jesus characterizes this motivation as "the deceitfulness of riches." These two negative contemporary influences provide a major hindrance, "choking" responsiveness to the Word and leading to personal unfruitfulness. We have frequently seen in our ministries how anxiety, particularly over material things, can distract an individual from absorbing and responding to God's Word.

Paralleling Matthew's record of this account is Mark 4:19, where Mark, using Peter as a primary resource, adds one more of the Savior's observations on distracting anxieties and the deceitfulness of riches—"the desires for other things entering in choke the word, and it becomes unfruitful." There are other remaining lusts besides lust of the eyes or materialism (for example, those cited earlier from 1 John 2:15-17), lust of the flesh—sexual and similar temptations, and lust for power—the pride of life. When anxiety is present in our lives, frequently these lusts are suppressed from consciousness, producing anxiety and hindering the effect of God's Word. If we refuse to look at the truth about these issues as spiritual choices, the consequences can be observed, not only in the spiritual realm, but in emotional and physical areas as well.

The third parallel passage in the Synoptic Gospels, Luke 8:14, includes the element of anxious "cares, riches, and pleasures of life" (the term *bios* is used here to indicate simple, basic pleasures, apparently including food and drink, sexual pleasures, and others), again hindering fruitfulness and maturity. In summary, Jesus' second major statement on anxiety, recorded by all the Synoptic Gospels, indicates how anxiety, particularly as it relates to the distractions of material and sensual pleasures, hinders a proper response to the Word of God and divinely designed fruitfulness.

It is not surprising that Luke, since he is a medical doctor, records a significant amount of what Jesus has to say about anxiety. For example, in Luke 10:41, the narrative about Jesus' interaction with Martha and Mary, Jesus confronts Martha to make her aware of her anxiety and agitation, saying, "Martha, you are worried and troubled about many things." Although a variety of cares had distracted Martha, producing agitation, in contrast, Mary has chosen the "one thing . . . needed": listening to and learning from Jesus. It is interesting in this passage to note the interplay between the term to care *(meli)* used of an object of care by Martha ("You do not care that my sister has left me to serve alone?"), and Martha's anxious care *(merimnao)* about many things. The term *meli* is generally used to suggest forethought and interest rather than anxiety. It is found in Matthew 22:16, Mark 4:38, Mark 12:14, Luke 10:40, John 10:13, John 12:6, Acts 18:17, and 1 Corinthians 9:9. In 1 Peter 5:7, it is also linked with the term for anxious care. Peter counsels "casting all your anxious care [*merimna*] upon Him, for He cares [*melei*] for you. It is His personal interest in the big things and little things of life that make it not only possible but imperative that we place our distracting cares and concerns upon Him. Another interesting facet of Luke's narrative about Jesus' interaction with Martha is that it is found in the context between the parable of the Good Samaritan in which the Samaritan cared for the needs of another (v. 10:34) and Jesus' instruction of His disciples in the prayer we commonly call "The Lord's Prayer," which includes requests for provision of daily needs (11:3), with the related parable instructing us to "ask, and it will be given you" (vv. 9-13). The point of this entire section from Luke is obvious. You need not be anxious and troubled about many things, for God can and will care for every need when we trust in Him and make Him a priority.

Luke continues his record of Jesus' discussion of anxiety by linking two concepts we have considered earlier, the warning against being anxious about a response to persecution (12:11), with the extended discourse of the Sermon on the Mount, perhaps repeated here later in Jesus' ministry (vv. 22, 25, 26). Luke adds a warning about anxiety from the final week of Jesus' life given during his series of discourses on the Mount of Olives. In the context of encouraging prayer and watchfulness and living in light of the Second Coming, He warns, "Take heed to yourselves lest your hearts be weighed down with carousing, drunkenness, and cares of this life, and that day come on you unexpectedly" (21:34). Several major factors in anxiety can be found in this warning, including the importance of the heart or inner person, the relationship between the distracting cares or worries of life and material and physical pleasures, and the importance of living in light of eternity rather than simply existentially, for the moment. This final statement from the Lord suggests the following points of application:

1. Awareness or insight is essential for dealing with anxiety.
2. Distracting anxiety involves a choice.
3. That choice involves the priority of living in either the light of eternity or the distraction of temporal life.
4. The distraction of temporal life involves preoccupation with either material or physical pleasures.

Anxiety As Written About by Paul

It is ironic that Paul, who probably, according to most biblical scholars, was unmarried, raises the issue of anxiety in the context of marriage (1 Corinthians 7). The verb *merimnao* is used three times in the extended section on the normal concerns of life (vv. 33–34). The issue here is not primarily negative versus positive, but just the reality of certain concerns which will distract us from other focuses. Paul sets the stage for his discussion of the benefits and drawbacks of marriage by making two observations. Number one, "If you do marry, you have not sinned." Number two, if you marry you will have trouble in this life (v. 28). The apostle's concern in this context is quite similar to that of Christ in the earlier passages cited. Paul is saying that all of us, married or single, need to live in light of eternity because "the form of this world is passing away" (v. 31). Cursory reading of verses 29 and 30 might lead some to conclude that Paul is exhorting married people to neglect their wives, those who suffered the loss of loved ones not to grieve, or those who have possessions not to use or enjoy them. Actually, Paul's point is not to condemn these things, but simply to point out the importance of establishing priorities and distinguishing the good from the best. In this context, Paul says, "I want you to be without care" (v. 32). The unmarried individual is free to be distracted toward the things of the Lord (v. 32) in contrast to the married individual, whose interests are divided and who thus must not only be concerned about the things of the Lord, but must take a certain concern or distraction toward material things in providing for the family. This is true both of husbands (v. 33) and of wives (v. 34). In concluding this discussion Paul acknowledges his motive: not to restrain marriage, but to promote serving God without "distraction." The point is marriage, family, providing for the needs of the household—all of these can distract from devotion to the Lord. It is imperative that, ,␣n in the decision to marry and establish a family, one consider the priority of the eternal over the temporal. It is also essential that we balance our concern for day-to-day provision of needs with the priority of spiritual and eternal factors. The two key factors are priority and balance.

The balance factor is underscored by three other uses, all positive. One of these, 1 Corinthians 12:25, indicates that members of the body, rather than being divided, should have "the same care for one another." Our concern for God and eternal things must be balanced by an evident concern for both strong and weak members of Christ's body. We should not be like the two individuals, the priest and the Levite in Luke 10, who passed up the "neighbor" on the road between Jerusalem and Jericho. Rather, our approach should be like that of the Good Samaritan, who was distracted to the point of taking the time to care for the needs of another. Paul clothes this concept in flesh and blood in Philippians 2:20, the second reference, by describing Timothy in positive terms as one "like-minded, who *will sincerely care*" for your welfare. Timothy, like-minded with Paul, was willing to be distracted in order to meet the needs of others in Christ's body. As such, he provides for us a practical example of how we are to care for others and their needs. A third illustration of this care is seen in Paul's personal testimony in defense of his ministry in 2 Corinthians 11:28, where he talks about how his life is compounded, not only by persecution, labor, hardship, and need, all of which are characterized as external things, but also by daily pressure upon me (which by inference is clearly internal) of "deep *concern* [*merimna*] for all the churches." Even in his zealous concern to preach the Gospel to unsaved people, Paul was distracted to care for local churches and the people within them. He, too, is the living epitome of priority and balance in dealing with anxiety. Although he was not distracted by sensual pleasures and materialism, Paul was distracted by caring genuinely for people.

Related New Testament Terms

The apostle Paul uses a number of related terms to describe aspects of this kind of care. One example is the term *spoude,* which primarily means "haste, zeal, diligence, earnest care," or "carefulness." While *merimna* denotes division or distraction, *spoude* has the idea of focus, watchful interest, and earnestness. *Spoude* is used in 2 Corinthians 7:11 and 12 of the Corinthians' concern to do what was right in the exercise of church discipline in obedience to Paul's instruction and in 2 Corinthians 8:16 of Titus and his companion's zeal for service to God. An intensive form of *melo, epimelimi* used for the Good Samaritan's care in Luke 10:34–35, described Paul's perspective on the overseer's care of the church (1 Tim. 3:5). Another related term, *phrone,* is used of this function in Hebrews 12:15. In Philippians 4, Paul deals directly with anxiety, discussing the priority of experiencing peace of mind and life in the thought life by having an appropriate mindset. In this context, Paul expresses his joy in the Philippians' care for him.

Their willingness to be distracted from their concerns in life to care for Paul's needs is set in the context of Paul's most extensive discussion of the subject of anxiety. Throughout the book of Philippians, the apostle has emphasized joy and rejoicing. As he concludes his letter to his beloved friends in Philippi (compare his love for them in 1:3–7), he encourages them to stand fast in the Lord (4:1), to be unified rather than divided (v. 2), to help each other (v. 3), to experience continual rejoicing (v. 4) and sweet reasonableness in responding to others (v. 5). Against this backdrop, he gives a strong negative command: "Be anxious for nothing" (v. 6). The thrust of his statement is *"stop* being anxious," implying the presence of anxiety over a wide variety of things. Certainly if the Philippians were like many of us today, they were concerned over many different things and perhaps anxiously distracted from their spiritual lives in the process.

Paul is careful not to tell them simply to remove anxiety. Rather, he suggests they replace it with prayer, supplication, and thanksgiving. These three related terms indicate personal interaction, verbalizing concerns and requests to God, asking Him to meet needs, and expressing appreciation for what He has done. The term *request,* in fact, indicates specific areas of concern and need, which should be voiced to God. The promised result of replacing distracting anxiety with this approach is the experience of the peace of God (v. 7) provided by the God of peace (v. 9). The importance of the unconscious mind as a factor in anxiety can be seen in Paul's promise that God's peace will, in a manner beyond human understanding, guard and protect their hearts and minds.

However, this promised protection from anxious thoughts does not preclude the responsibility to be thinking on those things that are honest, honorable, just, pure, lovely, of good report, virtuous, and praiseworthy (v. 8). Making the right choices about where we focus our minds is an important component in fighting anxiety. This "positive thinking" of verse 8 will lead to positive behaving (v. 9). The verbs in these two "think" (v. 8) and "do" (v. 9) verses are parallel. In other words, Paul instructs the Philippians to think about positive things, to practice those things they have learned, heard, and seen from him. Paul's promised result is fellowship with the God of peace. Thus, the key to mental and emotional health and even to physical health is to replace anxious thoughts with appropriate prayerful response to God, a choice of appropriate things on which to be concentrating or thinking, and a choice of the proper and appropriate Christian behaviors. From the term *promao* found in Romans 12:17 and 2 Corinthians 8:21 comes a similar idea of regard or paying attention to.

Other related New Testament terms besides those used by Paul include *tarasso,* which means "to stir up, disturb," or "throw into agitation" (used twenty-one times). A literal example is in John 5:4 and 7, the agitation of the waters of the pool of Bethesda. A normal use related to anxiety can be seen of the troubled state of Herod and the residents of Jerusalem at the report of the birth of the Messiah (Matt. 2:3) and in Mark 6:50 of the disciples when they saw Christ walking on the water. Intensified compounds of this word are used of Mary's feelings when Gabriel appeared to her (Luke 1:29), the impact of Paul and Silas on Philippi (Acts 16:20), of the normal grief of Christ at the death of Lazarus (John 11:33, 38), of Christ's feelings at the thought of betrayal by Judas (John 12:27), and of Christ's encouragement to his disciples not to be "troubled" or "afraid" (John 14:1, 27). Thus, the term has no negative moral connotation. It simply indicates internal agitation.

A similar term, *lupeo,* is used of the feelings of Epaphroditus (Phil. 2:26). Another term, *ekstasis,* is found in Mark 5:42 and Acts 3:10. Thus, a wide range of vivid terms with shades of meaning are used to show internal anxiety and agitation in the New Testament.

Peter's Perspective on Anxiety

A final perspective from Peter parallels instructions on anxiety as described by the Lord and as written about by Paul. This perspective is found in a short statement at the close of First Peter, following an extensive discussion of suffering adversity in the face of the hostile society in which first-century Christians lived. The major instruction of 1 Peter 5:6 is to accept circumstances humbly, trusting God ultimately to exalt us. The issue, as with other anxiety-focused passages such as Matthew 6, is God's sovereignty. Can we trust God, even when things go against us? Peter suggests we must. Following this call for submissive humility, Peter instructs us to choose "casting all your care upon Him," just what David describes in Psalm 37. To cast our cares upon Him involves a choice, taking a specific action. The reason for this action is clearly given. God cares, not just about our problems, but for us as individuals. Thus, all our cares, big ones and little ones and all those in between, including those that anxiously distract us, can be entrusted to Him. It seems evident that Peter's perspective here is colored, to some extent, by the input he received from the Lord and his Sermon on the Mount (Matt. 6), the sermon by the seaside (Mark 4, Matt. 13, Luke 8), and the Olivet discourse (Luke 21). In straightforward language, Peter calls for humble trust (v. 6), giving specific cares and distractions to the Lord through prayer (v. 7), and awareness of the priority of spiritual issues (vv. 8–11). It is, in fact, God's ultimate purpose to mature and firm, strengthen and establish us, in light of His overall sovereignty (vv. 10–11). An appropriate trust of the sovereign God demands that we handle the distracting and anxious cares of daily life in the right way.

Summary

We can make the following observations about what the New Testament teaches concerning anxiety.
1. The basic New Testament idea is that anxiety involves distraction or a distracting care.
2. Anxiety can be positive and negative, though the concept is primarily negative in Scripture.
3. Anxiety involves inappropriate responses in the mind or heart, the inner being.
4. Anxiety can include responses, motives, and emotions relative to material, sensual, and significant issues.
5. "Appropriate anxiety" involves choosing to be distracted from self to care for and focus on the needs of others or on God's work.
6. Inappropriate anxiety often produces stunted spiritual growth and leads to unfruitfulness.
7. Such anxiety is primarily a lack of faith.
8. Thus, anxiety involves a deficient response to the sovereignty of God and can be a product of perfectionism.
9. Anxiety involves the denial of God's personal care for us, especially in little things.
10. Anxiety is a choice, primarily a spiritual choice.
11. Anxiety often has a future component or preoccupation.

12. Anxiety can include concern over things appropriate (basic necessities) or inappropriate (for example, materialism).
13. One major technique in dealing with anxiety is a vital prayer life, communication and fellowship with God.
14. Such prayer includes taking all specific needs and concerns to God, rather than internalizing them or trying to figure out "what we can do about them."
15. However, this does not preclude our taking appropriate behavioral action steps.
16. One important action step is to rearrange the focus of our thought life onto those things which are appropriate.
17. The end result of handling anxiety appropriately is spiritual growth and maturity.
18. Another important result of handling anxiety appropriately is the ability to focus on spiritual issues as a priority, while maintaining balance.
19. This balance will manifest itself in appropriate concern about material things—family, and for others in the body of Christ.
20. Finally, the evidence from Jesus, Paul, and Peter is conclusive. It *is* possible for the person who handles anxiety biblically to experience worry-free living.

The Term *Fear*

One of the concepts most extensively dealt with in Scripture is fear. In fact, many more verses discuss fear than discuss anxiety. For purposes of distinction, we may observe that anxiety is seen as apprehension, dread, or unease; a distraction, often with indefinite or even nonexistent objects. Fear almost always seems to have a specific object, either stated or implied. Yet in Scripture the terms are often interchangeable, with little or no strong contrast, and at times both are seen to have an identified cause. There are approximately 330 references to fear throughout both the Old and New Testaments. There are many similarities and many contrasts between anxiety and fear. One similarity is that both involve control issues and, thus, faith issues. For example, Jacob expresses fear of his brother, Esau, in Genesis 32:11. This kind of fear of an object or person can be appropriate or inappropriate.

Fear *in the Old Testament*

The Hebrew *yirah* primarily means "to be afraid, to stand in awe, to fear." It is used of Jacob's human response to his brother in a life-threatening situation. It is also used by the angel of the Lord with Abraham: "Now I know that you *fear* God since you have not withheld your son, your only son, from me" (Gen. 22:12). Similarly, Jacob feared God at Bethel (Gen. 28:17). The Israelites feared God and trusted Him and Moses (Ex. 14:31). This is not simply honor or reverence for God, as some have implied. It includes this, but involves more. Perhaps the best way to summarize it is to say this Person (God or, in some cases, a powerful human) can control me and even crush me or do me harm; thus, I must respect and respond to this person or circumstance. Such fear may even include an element of dread (Deut. 2:25; 11:25).

Significantly, fear is the very first emotion mentioned in Scripture. It occurs in Genesis 3:10 in Adam's statement to God, immediately following his disobedience: "I was afraid because I was naked; and I hid myself." Here the Hebrew *yare* is used absolutely, without a direct object. Yet there was a cause for the fear. Similarly, in Genesis 19:30, Lot feared to do something, to live in Zoar. Twelve times in the Old Testament the noun form *to fear* appears, usually the fear of being before a superior being. It is used in Deuteronomy 4:34 of human response to God's mighty works, sovereignty, and destruction. It is used to describe the reaction of animals to men (Gen. 9:2), of the surrounding nations to God's power, the Israelite conquest (Deut. 11:25). Another noun for fear or reverence, *yare*, is used forty-five times in the Old Testament for a fear of God (Jon. 1:9), reverence toward God (Gen. 20:11), a fear of men (Deut. 2:25), a fear of objects (Isa. 7:25), the fear of situations or circumstances (Jon. 1:10).

Fear is often the English translation of the Hebrew *yera*, and sometimes also of the word *pachad*, ("quaking, horror"). In almost every instance, this word describes a circumstance in which the fearful individual is confronted with a sudden or already-present threat. This threat may be posed by God Himself, by a military power, or by physical danger. The subject of fear in the Old Testament is almost always man. Individuals may be fearful (Isaac in Gen. 26:7; Jacob in Gen. 32:7; Moses in Ex. 2:14; David in 1 Sam. 21:12; Nehemiah in Neh. 2:2). Groups of people also can be permeated by fear (the tribe of Esau in Deut. 2:4; the Ammonites in 2 Sam. 10:19; Israelites in many passages).

Examining the nature of fear involves a focus on its object as well as a reason for it. At times fear is of a death (Gen. 26:7; Neh. 6:10–13), a loss of a significant family member such as a wife (Gen. 31:31) or child (2 Sam. 14:15), a fear of disaster (Ps. 23:4), a fear of enslavement (Gen. 43:18), a fear of misfortune (Job 6:21), or a fear of some sudden terror (Prov. 3:25). Most of these Old Testament instances of fear have a much more definite object and reason than anxiety. Thus, "the starting point of fear is especially a threat to life, living space, all the spheres that give life meaning."[1]

Positive instruction of the fear of God is based on His sovereignty and His love. The term *to fear* is linked with the word "to love," *ahav*, and *rabaq*, "to cleave to." In Deuteronomy 10:12 and 20 and 13:4, responsive fear will drive us to love God because of His love for us and to cling to Him because of His sovereignty over us. In Proverbs 2:1–5, the fear of God is linked carefully with knowledge, *daat;* insight, *tabunah;* and wisdom, *hochmach*. Thus, Solomon underscores from a divine perspective the importance of gaining insight into the origin of our fears, knowledge of what to do with them, and the skill or wisdom to apply the knowledge.

Fear of the Lord also includes a moral component, such as steering us away from evil (Job 1:1, 8; Ps. 34:11, 14; Prov. 3:7), and motivating us to hate sin (Prov. 28) and avoid sin (Prov. 23:17). Thus, to fear God is to walk uprightly (Prov. 14:2), gaining honor, success, and protection in life (Prov. 22:4). Fear of God lengthens life (Prov. 10:27; 14:27) and provides security, confidence and refuge (Prov. 14:26; 19:23).

The exhortation "Fear not!" is found throughout the Old Testament. This is one of the most common ways of expressing reassurance of God's presence and help. The phrase is often spoken by God's spokesmen (Ex. 14:13; Jer. 42:11; Isa. 41:10, 13) or by people to each other (2 Sam. 9:7).

The term *pachad* is often used of anxious uncertainty and disquiet (Deut.

28:65; Job 3:25). It is contrasted with shalom or peace (Job 15:21; 21:9). Often such terrors and anxiety arise in the night (Ps. 91:5; Song of Sol. 3:8) or may have specific origin such as fear of enemies (Ps. 64:1; Job 39:22).

A strong contrast is drawn between the fear of God and fears of circumstances or death. The fear of God is an appropriate response and consistent with trust in contrast to the fear of circumstances or even death.

Throughout the Old Testament, a right relationship with God can lay personal fears to rest. Personal fears are often admitted to in Scripture. In fact, Job, throughout his discourse, admits to fear of God and of circumstances (Job 4:14; 9:34–35; 11:15; 31:34). Early in Israel's life, Moses instructed the Israelites to "walk in His ways and fear Him" (Deut. 8:6; see also 6:2, 13, 24; 10:12, 20; 13:4).

The Book of Psalms provides a great deal of encouragement and instruction on the subject of fear. Fear is related to trust and worship of God (Ps. 2:11; 5:7; 15:4; 19:9). God is also seen as the source of encouragement and protection and the answer for personal fears. The familiar "I will fear no evil; / For You are with me" (Ps. 23:4) underscores God's protection against all fears. In Psalm 31 David describes a wide range of fears. He experienced fear resulting from abandonment by his friends and acquaintances (vv. 11–12); he feared the verbal and physical assaults of enemies (vv. 13, 15). The contrast is with fear of God (v. 19), which leads to a personal trust (v. 14–15):

> But as for me, I trusted in You, O LORD;
> I say, 'You are my God,'
> My times are in Your hand;
> Deliver me from the hand of my enemies,
> And from those who persecute me.

Trust in God as refuge can eliminate fear and disastrous circumstances (Ps. 46:1–2). In fact, this Psalm points to fearlessness as a choice ("Therefore we *will* not fear . . ."). Whenever fear is present, the appropriate response should be to choose to trust in God (Ps. 56:3–4). Giving God the fear and respect due Him is an appropriate part of wisdom (Ps. 90:11–12). Solomon echoes this idea in Proverbs 1:33: those who listen to God will "be secure, without fear of evil." Thus, there is no need to fear sudden terror or ultimate desolation since our confidence and protection is in God (Prov. 3:25–26). The wisdom of walking with God and trusting in God can even preclude fear which robs us of sleep (3:24). Thirteen times in Proverbs the fear of the Lord is recognized as a component of wisdom. This is also seen in Solomon's concluding or summary statement in Ecclesiastes 12:13, "Fear God and keep His commandments."

Isaiah the prophet underscores God's words of encouragement relative to fear. Three times in Isaiah 41, he uses God's protection and encouragement as a motivation to "fear not" (vv. 10, 13, 14). The powerful Creator is present; therefore, there is no need to fear. What significant implications for believers today! Over and over, Isaiah exhorts the nation, "Fear not; stop being afraid." The other prophets echo this response (Jer. 30:10; Ezekiel 3:9; Joel 2:21; Zeph. 3:16; Hagg. 2:5; Zech. 8:13, 15).

Fear *in the Literature of Biblical Times*

One of the most common words in the Greek language is the word *phobos*. Many students of the Greek language draw correlation between this term *phobos* and *phobe*, the word for the mane of a horse, suggesting the idea of "hair raising." The field of medicine has long documented the physiological reaction of hair rising in response to fear, though the connection is not certain. Another concept involved in this word is to be startled and to run away, the idea of flight. In fact, many of the Greek poets, including Homer, used *phobos* to indicate a fear response that led to flight. Significantly, the name for one of the moons of Mars is *phobos*, perhaps so designated because of its continued flight through the heavens.

A related word, *deos*, seems to carry the idea of fear or apprehension, while *phobos* is used more of sudden and violent fear, fright, or panic. These are terms used in the New Testament in addition to those cited for anxiety. The verb form, *phobao* can mean "to terrify" or "put to flight," and in the middle voice it can mean "to flee." In fact, at times it is even used of apprehension. Plato and Aristotle used the term for strong physical emotion and even for anxiety. Demosthenes pointed out that *phobos* can lead to confusion, or *ekplaksis*. Clearly, there is a great deal of overlap between what we might today call fear and anxiety. Much of the Greek material is wrapped around the god Phobos, who is listed just after Zeus in the Greek pantheon. This god was seen as a powerful deity and drawn as a symbol of a lion or a serpent on the shields of Greek warriors. Phobos, according to Homer, was the god of terror, the martial god who struck fear into the hearts of all with whom he came in contact. These extrabiblical considerations give understanding of how New Testament writers may have grasped the meaning of the terms they used in Scripture.

The essence of fear, thus, is a reaction to man's encounter with force, particularly a force more powerful than himself. A wide scale of responses can be documented, ranging from spontaneous terror to anxiety, honor, respect, and submission. For the Greeks, fear was to be avoided and the absence of fear was a worthwhile object. Fear was seen as immobilizing, and in Greek tragedy, the dread of the unknown future played a key role in fear. Thoughtful individuals should not be troubled by fear, which was seen as similar to the terror of a helpless animal (a common metaphor in Homer). The Greeks would pray to their gods in order to deal with fear. The Oracle at Delphi contains a strong motif of fear; its message contains an acknowledgment of "the might, or power of fear."

The foundation for a great deal of the New Testament evidence on fear can be seen in the Greek literature of the day. Not only did the Greeks fear the gods' powers over nature, they also feared governmental authorities and powers. The Greek physiological perspective on fear involved the cooling off of the body through the lack of blood. Physiological symptoms were often cited, such as cramps, trembling, pain, and agony. Psychological responses such as pathos, emotion, and desire or pleasure *(lupē, phobos, epithumia,* and *Hedonae)* were designated by the Greeks as the four basic emotions: grief, fear, desire, and pleasure. The Greeks demanded fearlessness of the thinking man and presented cognitive rearranging of the thought life as the best antidote to fear. Today we call it cognitive restructuring. Plato rejected the fear of death, but taught the fear of wrongdoing.

The Greeks rejected emotional fear, yet this rejection does not always parallel their use of terms for fear. Perhaps this reflected a denial of fear as an emotion.

Josephus, one of the great Hebrew chroniclers, used the term *phobos* 150 times and *phobamoi* 70 times. He talked of fear of danger, fear of death, and anxiety about life and its circumstances. His use of *phobamoi* is not usually related to God.

Fear *in the New Testament*

In the New Testament, the word *phobos* is used in noun or verb form about 160 times. The major uses are found in the Gospels and Acts. As a rule, the term is used in a general sense and often appears in specific people. People might fear to do certain things (Matt. 1:20), be afraid that certain things might occur (Acts 5:26; Acts 23:10), or fear specific individuals (Mark 6:20; Luke 19:21; Acts 9:26). Sometimes fear is simply a response to circumstances (John 19:8; Acts 16:38).

Generally, in the New Testament, fear involves the general threats of life and is not specifically related to any concerns of Christians. Like anxiety, there are good and bad senses of fear. For example, a distraction to care for the needs of others is good, while hampering and distracting anxiety over the cares and pleasures of life is bad. The fear of God, especially as it relates to trust is good. The fear of circumstances, which is contrasted with trust in God to protect and care for us in our circumstances, is portrayed as bad.

One of the most important senses of fear is in response to the mighty works or miracles of Jesus. On numerous occasions, both the multitudes and the disciples responded with fear. This parallels the fear of God in the Old Testament and strongly underscores the deity of Christ.

Luke, the physician, makes the largest number of references of any New Testament book to fear, twenty in twenty-four chapters. Seven of these are found in the extended account of the birth and early life of Christ, including the angelic encounters with Zacharias and Mary (note that Matthew also documents the "fear not" injunction given Joseph by the angel and the "fear not" of the angel to the shepherds on the night of Christ's birth). In Luke 5:7–8, in the description of Jesus' initial call to Peter, Andrew, James, and John, Christ miraculously provides a huge quantity of fish after a night of fruitless fishing so that the boat is about to sink. Peter's response is significant; he falls at Jesus' knees and says, "Depart from me, for I am a sinful man, O Lord." He is literally astonished and terrified, as are his partners, the sons of Zebedee. Jesus' instruction, "Do not be afraid, From now on you will catch men" (v. 10), not only lays Peter's fear to rest, but gives his entire life a new direction. Thus, fear serves to bring about submission, faith, and obedience.

The Gospels point out how fear and faith are linked, just as anxiety and faith are linked (Matt. 6:30). In Mark 4, Matthew 8, and Luke 8, Jesus miraculously stills the storm on the lake. Mark describes the event by noting that there are other little boats, as well as the boat in which Jesus and His disciples are traveling. The reason for this is to demonstrate that there are other witnesses: The disciples do not dream or hallucinate that this happened; and there is a genuine storm of wind (4:37). The term used by Mark denotes a whirlwind; his account comes directly from Peter, who is an eyewitness. As waves beat into the boat, it fills; this is a desperate situation! And at this point, Jesus is sleeping on a pillow in the stern of the boat. The disciples awaken Him and say, "Teacher, do You not care that we are perishing?" In other words, we are going down! Jesus stands and rebukes the wind and the sea—the terms we translate "Peace, be still" literally say "Be muzzled" as one might speak to a dog. The ferocious wind suddenly, dramatically drops to a great calm. Turning to His disciples, Jesus says, "Why are you so fearful? How is it that you have no faith?" (vv. 38–41). In the case of anxiety in Matthew 8, Jesus says that their anxiety demonstrates "little faith" (v. 26). Having been intensely fearful of the elements which threatened their lives (and humanly speaking, rightly so), having seen Jesus' divine power to still the storm, they fear Him even more intensely. Luke records the question, "Where is your faith?" The disciples are both afraid and amazed. Their response is quite similar to that of the witnesses to Jesus' healing of the paralyzed man (Luke 5:18–26). There the response to the circumstances they had seen is documented as being amazed, glorifying God, and being filled with fear. A similar response takes place at the raising of the widow's son (Luke 7:16) and the liberating of the demon-possessed man at Gerasenes (Luke 8:37).

Following the demonstration of Jesus' divine power and the response of fear, Luke documents a significant discourse before a large crowd of people, where Jesus warns of the evil influence of the Pharisees (Luke 12). He cautions his friends not to fear humans who simply have the power to take away temporal life (v. 4), but rather to fear God who has authority over eternity as well as time (v. 5). Three times in verse 5 he uses the word *fear,* beginning with "Him whom you should fear." This fear of God, coupled with awareness of His power (v. 5) and His personal concern, even to the numbering of the very hairs of your head" (vv. 6–7), should lead us away from fear of circumstances and provides a basis for Jesus' encouraging words, "Fear not."

It is significant to note the connection between fear and self-concept, which is underscored by Jesus' statement, "You are of more value than many sparrows." The context is a personal relationship with a powerful yet caring God. Later in the discourse, Jesus summarizes by assuring "Do not fear, little flock . . . it is your Father's good pleasure to give you the kingdom" (v. 32). Our connection with God's ultimate rule and plan gives us a basis to choose not to fear.

Two other references to fearing God are found in the context of the unjust judge (Luke 18:4) and the thief on the cross (Luke 23:40). The final reference to fear is found in Christ's description of His return in power and glory and a preview of the tribulation in which He says, "men's hearts [will be] failing them from fear . . . for the powers of heaven will be shaken" (Luke 21:26). Statements of the other Gospels relative to fear show significant parallels with these.

Luke also authored the book of Acts, which contains seven additional references to fear. Several of these indicate a fearful response in light of God's power, evidenced by God's dramatically bringing the church into existence (2:43), protecting it from persecution and pollution (Acts 5:5, 11), and bringing others to faith (Acts 19:27). Two references are to the concept of fearing the Lord (Acts 9:31; 13:16), which are found in appeals to God-fearing Jews. Acts 27:24 is a special case in which, in the face of storm and impending shipwreck, God personally encourages the apostle traveling to Rome with the words, "Do not be afraid, Paul." God tells Paul that no one will lose their lives, though the ship will be lost. Several observations arise from the use of fear in Acts. When God's work is evidenced in the lives of His people, fear of God will be a by-product. God personally cares that we not fear in adverse circumstances. Fear should be the response to God's attitude toward and action against sin by His people.

Several times during the Upper Room Discourse Jesus encourages His disciples not to be afraid (John 14:27). The term used there, *deilia*, denotes a spirit of cowardice or timidity. This word is never used positively in the New Testament.

Fear *in Paul's Writings*

The apostle Paul deals with the subject of fear in three major ways. First, he encourages an appropriate fear of God. One mark of lost and spiritually blind individuals is a lack of fear of God (Rom. 3:18). Christians, too, need to cultivate fear of God as opposed to arrogance (Rom. 11:20), and this fear should lead to appropriate fear for God-given governmental authorities (Rom. 13:7). It should also lead to submission to one another in the body of Christ (Eph. 5:21), and specifically in a submissive, obedient attitude toward those for whom we work (Eph. 6:5, where the context is the attitude of first-century slaves). Public rebuke for sin, particularly on the part of leaders, should motivate all Christians to fear, and personal good works should be done "with fear and trembling" (Phil. 2:12). The contrast between God and immoral idolatry should motivate us to personal purity "in the fear of God" (2 Cor. 7:1). The Corinthians evidenced this in their response to the individual from their assembly who had been immoral and toward whom Paul had instructed them to exercise discipline. He says they did it in fear (7:11, 15). Thus, fear of God and of the consequences of disobedience should motivate us to purity, to good works, to submissive attitudes toward one another, and toward an appreciation for God's sovereign working in our lives.

The second major area Paul addresses in terms of fear is more personal in character. The apostle explains his own fearfulness in the presence of the believers in Corinth (1 Cor. 2:3) and expresses his fears relative to their being corrupted and misled doctrinally or engaging in divisive disorder (2 Cor. 11:3; 12:20). These fears expressed by the apostle seem to parallel his statements about the anxious care for the churches referred to earlier.

The third major thrust of Paul's expression relative to fear is that Christians do not need to have the same kind of fear regarding circumstances or the world. For example, in Romans 8:15, Paul points out that believers, led by the spirit of God, need no longer be in bondage to fear. Fear enslaves; yet, believers are indwelt by the very presence of God, as represented in the third Person of the trinity, God the Holy Spirit. Furthermore, we are people of significance because we "have received the spirit of adoption," giving us a close personal relationship with Him as represented in the phrase "Abba, Father." Thus, our lives need not be permeated by fear. Furthermore, there is no need to fear adversity in proclaiming the reality of Christ to those who reject Him. Though Paul was imprisoned for his preaching of the Gospel of Christ, he was encouraged that, despite his imprisonment, many of the brethren had become extremely confident and were "more bold to speak the word without fear" (Phil. 1:14). In addition, Paul encourages the sometimes timid Timothy with the reminder that "God has not given us a spirit of fear, but of power and of love and of a sound mind" (2 Tim. 1:7). The term used here for fear, *deilia* again, indicates cowardice or timidity and parallels the word *phobos* used by Paul elsewhere. Paul's reminder of God's power at work in his life

(v. 6) is designed to not only alleviate his attitude of timidity and replace it with an awareness of God's power and appreciation for God's love and a sound mind, but also to promote his witness for Christ, even in the face of adversity and persecution (v. 8).

In 2 Corinthians 7:5, Paul does admit to personal struggles: "Outside were conflicts, inside were fears." His vulnerability here gives believers today an encouraging point of identification.

The use of the terms for fear in the general epistles and revelation parallels many of the characteristics of fear brought out by Paul: the absence of the fear of God by apostates (Jude 12), the necessity for believers fearing God (1 Pet. 2:17; Rev. 11:18; 19:5), the importance of fear toward authority figures (1 Pet. 2:18; 3:2) and in light of spiritual dangers (Heb. 4:1; Jude 23). In Hebrews 13:6, the author asserts, "I will not fear. What can man do to me?" Our love relationship with God should remove fears (1 John 4:18). Personal fears of the authors of Scripture are presented secondhand of Moses (Heb. 12:21) and firsthand of John the apostle (Rev. 1:17). John also is reminded to "fear none of those things which you saw."

Summary Observations about Fear

1. Fear is primarily a response to power.
2. It indicates a desire to flee.
3. In contrast to anxiety, fear generally has a specific object, though there is not a consistent distinction between anxiety and fear in Scripture.
4. Fear can have either a positive or a negative impact.
5. Many unbelievers and apostates are not marked by fear of God.
6. Those who trust God are to fear Him, though this does not in any way eliminate the close, loving relationship with God which eliminates other fears.
7. Fear is also appropriate in certain relationships with those in positions of human authority.
8. Fear is also appropriate as a response to spiritual danger. At times, we may even fear in the sense of being concerned about negative events or failures in the lives of God's children.
9. Yet, the general attitude of Christians is not to be a "spirit of fear." Fear of circumstances and adversities or a spirit of timidity or giving up are not to be marks of the Christians.
10. Love frees us from fear to fellowship with God, providing freedom and openness in relationships.
11. Fear of God should motivate us to purity of life and walk.
12. In essence, fear can either be the antithesis of faith or a part of faith. It is the antithesis of faith when it is directed toward circumstances rather than God. It is a component of faith when it moves us to trust in and submit to Him.
13. The implications for believers are obvious. We must make the choices which will open the way for God to replace our fears of circumstances with a fear of and trust in Him, which will lead to appropriate submission and humility.

For Further Reading

Abbott-Smith, G. *A Manual Greek Lexicon of the New Testament*. 3rd ed. Edinburgh: T. & T. Clark, 1937.

Archer, Gleason L., and G. C. Chirichigno. *Old Testament Quotations in the New Testament: A Complete Survey*. Chicago: Moody, 1983.

Arndt, William F. and Wilbur Gingrich. *A Greek-English Lexicon of the New Testament*. Grand Rapids, Michigan: Zondervan, 1952.

Bannister, Sir Roger. *Brain's Clinical Neurology*. 6th ed. New York: Oxford University Press, 1985.

Blass, Friedrich and Albert DeBrunner. *A Greek Grammar of the New Testament and Other Early Christian Literature*. 9th ed. Trans. by Robert W. Funk. Chicago: University of Chicago, 1961.

Botterweck, G. Johannes, and Helmer Ringgren, eds. *Theological Dictionary of the Old Testament*. Trans. John T. Willis. Grand Rapids, Michigan: Eerdmans, 1978. Vol. 1–2.

Carlson, Neal R. *Physiology of Behavior*. 3rd Edition. Boston: Allyn and Bacon, 1986.

Carson, Robert C., James N. Butcher, and James C. Coleman. *Abnormal Psychology and Modern Life*. 8th ed. Illinois: Scott, Foresman, 1987.

Chafer, Lewis Sperry. *Systematic Theology*. 8 vols. Grand Rapids, Michigan: Zondervan, 1981.

Cremer, Hermann. *Biblico-Theological Lexicon of New Testament Greek*. Trans. William Urwick. New York: Charles Scribner's Sons, 1895.

Dana, H. E., and Julius R. Mantey. *A Manual Grammar of the Greek New Testament*. New York: MacMillan, 1957.

Davidson, A. B. *Hebrew Syntax*. Edinburgh: T & T Clark, 1901.

Davidson, Benjamin. *Analytical Hebrew and Chaldee Lexicon*. Grand Rapids, Michigan: Zondervan, 1970.

Deissmann, Adolph. *Light from the Ancient East*. Trans. Lionel R. M. Strachan. Grand Rapids, Michigan: Baker Book House, 1965.

Edersheim, A. *The Life and Times of Jesus the Messiah*. 2 vols. Grand Rapids, Michigan: Eerdmans, 1972.

Eichrodt, Walther. *Theology of the Old Testament*. 2 vols. Trans. J. Baker. Philadelphia: Westminster, 1967.

Englishman's Greek Concordance of the New Testament. Rev. George W. Vigram, Grand Rapids, Michigan: Zondervan, 1982.

Flournoy, Richard L., et al. *100 Ways to Obtain Peace*. Grand Rapids, Michigan: Baker Book House, 1986.

Ganong, William F. *Review of Medical Physiology*. 13th ed. Los Altos, California: Appleton and Lange, 1987.

Gatz, Arthur J. *Clinical Neuroanatomy and Neurophysiology.* 3rd ed. Philadelphia: F. A. Davis, 1966.

Gesenius, William. *A Hebrew and English Lexicon to the Old Testament.* 2nd ed. New York: Oxford, 1959.

Gesenius, William. *Hebrew Grammar.* Ed. E. Kautzsch. Rev. A. E. Cowley. Oxford: Clarendon, 1910.

Harris, R. Laird, et al. *Theological Wordbook of the Old Testament.* 2 vols. Chicago: Moody, 1980.

Harrison, R. K. *Introduction to the Old Testament.* Grand Rapids, Michigan: Eerdmans, 1969.

Hatch, Edwin, and Henry Redpath. *A Concordance to the Septuagint and Other Greek Versions of the Old Testament.* 3 vols. Grand Rapids, Michigan: Baker Book House, 1983.

Herink, Richie. *The Psychotherapy Handbook.* New York: New American Library, 1980.

Kaplan, Harold I., and Benjamin J. Sadock. *Comprehensive Textbook of Psychiatry/IV.* Vol. 1, 4th ed. Baltimore: Williams & Wilkins, 1984.

Kaplan, Harold I., and Benjamin J. Sadock. *Modern Synopsis of Comprehensive Textbook of Psychiatry/IV.* 4th ed. Baltimore: Williams & Wilkins, 1981.

Katzung, Bertram G. *Basic and Clinical Pharmacology.* 3rd ed. Los Altos, California: Appleton & Lange, 1987.

Kittel, Gerhard, and Gerhard Friedrich, eds. *Theological Dictionary of the New Testament.* Ed. and trans. Geoffrey Bromiley. Grand Rapids, Michigan: Eerdmans, 1971. 8 vols.

Kittel, Rudolf. *Biblica Hebraica.*

Klatzky, Roberta L. *Human Memory: Structures and Processes.* San Francisco: W. H. Freeman, 1975.

Kolb, Lawrence C. *Modern Clinical Psychiatry.* 8th ed. Philadelphia: W. B. Saunders, 1973.

Meier, Paul D., F. B. Minirth, and Frank Wichern. *Introduction to Psychology and Counseling.* Grand Rapids, Michigan: Baker Book House, 1982.

Minirth, Frank B. *Christian Psychiatry.* Old Tappan, New Jersey: Revell, 1977.

Minirth, Frank B., and Paul D. Meier. *Happiness Is a Choice.* Grand Rapids, Michigan: Baker Book House, 1988.

Minirth, F. B., P. D. Meier, and S. V. Skipper. *100 Ways to Live a Happy and Successful Life.* Grand Rapids, Michigan: Baker Book House, 1988.

Moulton, James H., and George Milligan. *The Vocabulary of the Greek Testament.* Grand Rapids, Michigan: Eerdmans, 1972.

Ryrie, Charles C. *The Ryrie Study Bible.* King James Version. Chicago: Moody, 1978.

Solomon, Philip, and Vernon D. Patch. *Handbook of Psychiatry.* 3rd ed. Los Altos, California: Lange Medical Publications, 1974.

————. *A Grammar of the Greek New Testament in the Light of Historical Research.* New York: Hodder and Stoughton, 1919.

————. *Word Pictures in the New Testament.* Nashville, Tennessee: Broadman, IV.

————. *Biblical Theology of the New Testament.* Chicago: Moody Press, 1959.

Trench, Robert C. *Synonyms of the New Testament*. Marshallton, Delaware: The National Foundation for Christian Education, 1950.

Unger, Merrill F. *Genesis-Song of Solomon*. Vol. 1. *Unger's Commentary on the Old Testament*. Chicago: Moody, 1981.

_____. *Unger's Bible Handbook*. Chicago: Moody Press, 1966.

Vine, W. E. *Expository Dictionary of New Testament Words*. 4 vols. Old Tappan, New Jersey: Revell, 1940.

Weingreen, J., M.A., Ph.D. *A Practical Grammer for Classical Hebrew*. Oxford: Clarenden, 1963.

Young, Robert. *Young's Analytical Concordance of the Bible*. Grand Rapids, Michigan: Eerdmans, 1969.

Notes

Chapter 1. What This Book Can (and Can't) Do for You
1. Ephesians 4:26.
2. Ephesians 4:31.

Chapter 2. The Hidden Emotion in "The Age of Anxiety"
1. Rollo May, *The Meaning of Anxiety* (New York: Norton, 1977), 205.
2. 1 John 1:9 TLB.
3. Psalm 103.
4. Philippians 3:13 TLB.
5. Charlotte Elliott, "Just As I Am," *The Broadman Hymnal* (Nashville: Broadman, 1940), 162.
6. Philippians 3:14.

Chapter 3. Eight Myths: "You'll Get Over It"
1. Harold Kaplan, Alfred Freedman, and Benjamin J. Saddock, eds., *Comprehensive Textbook of Psychiatry,* 2nd ed. (Baltimore: Williams and Wilkins, 1975), 785. Source: Dr. Thomas J. Holmes. From *The New York Times,* 10 June 1973.
2. Ruth 4:15.
3. Hebrews 13:5; Deuteronomy 31:6, 8; Joshua 1:5.
4. Ephesians 6:11.
5. Matthew 6:25–34.
6. James 5:16.
7. Mark 4:35–40.

Chapter 4. Who's Apt to Be Anxious?
1. Roy Grinker, "Perspectives on Normality," *Archives of General Psychiatry,* 1967), 17:257.
2. Frank B. Minirth and Paul D. Meier, *Happiness Is a Choice* (Grand Rapids, Michigan: Baker Book House, 1978), 55.
3. Luke 10:41 TLB.
4. Frank Minirth, et al., *The Workaholic and His Family* (Grand Rapids, Michigan: Baker Book House, 1981), 59–64.
5. Frank B. Minirth and Paul D. Meier, *How to Beat Burnout* (Chicago: Moody Press), 26–32.
6. Lucille Forer, with Henry Still, *The Birth Order Factor* (New York: David McKay, 1976), 11.

Chapter 5. Over the Brink
1. Thomas L. Horn, "Agoraphobia," *American Family Physician* 32 (July 1985): 165–173.

2. Neal Olshan and Julie Wang, *Everything You Wanted to Know about Phobias but Were Afraid to Ask* (New York: Beaufort Books, 1981), 214–220.
3. Minirth, et al., *The Workaholic,* 12.
4. Matthew 11:30.

Chapter 6. The Coverups: Defense Mechanisms
1. Jeremiah 17:9.
2. Proverbs 4:23.
3. Jeremiah 17:10; Psalm 139:23; Proverbs 21:2.
4. Psalm 19:14.
5. Psalm 139:23–24.
6. Matthew 12:34; Luke 6:45.
7. Matthew 15:19.
8. Barclay Martin, *Anxiety and Neurotic Disorders* (New York: John Wiley & Sons, 1971), 91.
9. Proverbs 14:15.
10. Genesis 12:11–20.
11. Proverbs 21:2.
12. Philippians 3:17.
13. 1 Samuel 18.
14. 1 Samuel 18:7.

Chapter 7. Self-Help or Professional Care?
1. Cynthia Joyce Rowland, *The Monster Within* (Grand Rapids, Michigan: Baker Book House, 1984), 84.
2. "A Deadly Feast and Famine," *Newsweek,* 7 Mar. 1983, 59–60.
3. *Quick Reference to the Diagnostic Criteria from DSM-III-R* (The American Psychiatric Association, 1987), 63–4.
4. Rowland, *Monster,* 96.
5. Ibid., 88–9.
6. James 3:2.

Chapter 8. Eight Ways to Prevent Anxiety
1. John 14:27.
2. Psalm 103:12.
3. J. E. Rankin, "Tell It to Jesus," *Broadman Hymnal,* 110.
4. 1 Samuel 16:23.
5. Matthew 6:34.
6. 2 Kings 6:14–17.
7. Philippians 4:6.
8. Hebrews 4:12, 3:13.
9. See Albert Ellis and Robert A. Harper, *A New Guide to Rational Living* (Englewood Cliffs: New Jersey: Prentice-Hall, 1961).
10. John 8:32.

Chapter 9. The Balanced Lifestyle
1. Fred Hooper, *The Counselor,* March 1986.
2. Frank Minirth, Paul Meier, and Richard Flournoy, *Sweet Dreams* (Richardson, Texas: Today Publishers, 1985), 14.
3. 1 Kings 19:1–9.